T0130194

Broken Healer

A Story of Healing
Through Brokeness

Daniel and Miriam Pope

WestBow
PRESS
A DIVISION OF THOMAS NELSON

ISBN: 978-1-4497-6353-4 (sc)
ISBN: 978-1-4497-6354-1 (e)

WestBow Press books may be ordered through booksellers or by contacting:

WestBow Press
A Division of Thomas Nelson
1663 Liberty Drive
Bloomington, IN 47403
www.westbowpress.com
1-(866) 928-1240

Library of Congress Control Number: 2012915175

Printed in the United States of America

WestBow Press rev. date: 09/20/2012

Contents

- All praise to God, the Father of our Lord Jesus Christ. God is our merciful Father and the source of all comfort. He comforts us in all our troubles so that we can comfort others. When they are troubled, we will be able to give them the same comfort God has given us.

-2 Corinthians 1:3-4 NLT

Acknowledgments

Thank you God, Jesus and Holy Spirit, no words can describe how much you mean to us, so may our lives reflect it.

To our parents, this book is dedicated to you. Thank you for your prayers, love and support. We are truly honored to be called your children.

To Uncle Bill, who spent countless days and nights making baby bottles, changing nappies (diapers), watching "High Five" and listening to the "The Wiggles" C D over and over again. You will never know how much we really needed you.

To the Carlos, thanks for being there at the right place, at the right time.

Thank you to all the employees and board of the Ottumwa Water Works for your generosity.

Finally, a BIG thank you to First Church of the Open Bible in Ottumwa, Iowa, you became the hands, feet and body of Jesus for us! You will always have a special place in our hearts.

Foreword

I had the privilege of being part of Dan and Miriam's (my sister) household on and off for nearly two years. They had kindly invited me to live in their house while my fiancée Bridget, (Dan's niece), finished her degree at a college nearby. Bridget and I had met at Dan and Miriam's wedding in Northern Ireland a few years previously, so to start with, I owe a great debt to them for getting married!

Faith, in Biblical terms, is not defined by circumstances. Rather it is faith that is present with belief and dependence through every season. This is the kind of faith I see alive in Dan and Miriam. Whether waiting for a post operation report or playing with the kids in the backyard, their faith in who God says He is remains. The extent of their faith is not dependent on the changing seasons of life but upon the unchanging promises of God.

Whilst living with Dan and Miriam we journeyed through many different seasons as a household. We shared in times of laughter and celebration, and also in times of heartache and hardship. Amidst seasons of dark uncertainty and pain, we saw the brightness of God's faithfulness, strength and peace. In times where our present reality cast a shadow of hopelessness over us, we witnessed together God's provision again and again.

Will Herron
Rend Collective Experiment

Faithful

There's no words that
You've spoken, That
haven't brought hope
No promise You've made
That You haven't fulfilled
Faithful Jesus, An offering
of praise I bring to You

Such grace that no man
Could ever repay
Patience that outlives
The doubts in my head
Faithful Jesus, An offering
of praise I bring to You

Surrounded by gifts of love
You express in life the
depth of Your love

Jesus, I will put my hope
in You, No idols compare
to who You are, all You've
given, I live to honor and
worship You, Be like a
window to who You are,
all You've given to me

You're Faithful to the end
There's no words that
You've spoken, That
haven't brought hope
No promise You've made
That You haven't fulfilled
Faithful Jesus, An offering
of praise I bring to You[1]

Introduction

It was a typical hot and humid late August Iowa morning. We packed a picnic lunch and headed to a friend's pond. Upon arrival we laid out our blanket under the shade of a tree and as Miriam reclined to the enjoyment of a book, I took Caelan (7) and Rian (4) to the edge of the pond where the ferocious fishing competition was about to begin.

In the heat of battle as the sweat dripped off our chins, I was trying to remove the hook out of the mouth of a bluegill that Rian had caught when one of the needles from its dorsal fin pierced my hand. Instantly I dropped the fish and yelled, "Ouch!"

As the blood trickled down my hand, Rian took one look and said, "I don't want to fish anymore."

I tried to convince him that as long I was the one who handled the fish there would be no way he could get hurt. He hung his head and walked away.

Do we get pierced and wounded in life? The answer to that is a resounding, "YES!" In those moments we have a choice - do we allow Jesus to handle the situation and come to our rescue or do we hang our heads, give up and walk away?

Caelan understood that I would be faithful to my word and that every time she caught a fish, I would be the one to handle it. She caught ten fish that day and when Rian finally realized that he would be protected by his father's hands, he picked up his fishing pole and began to fish once again.

A few weeks later the Holy Spirit reminded me of that moment with Rian. In my spirit I heard the Lord say, "That's what I have done for you. I allowed myself to be pierced and wounded so that you would be healed."

Isaiah prophesied about this very fact,

"But He was pierced for our transgressions, He was crushed for our iniquities; the punishment that brought us peace was on Him, and by his wounds we are healed."

-Isaiah 53:5 NIV

Perhaps you are in a place in your life right now where you feel pain, hurt, loss, discouragement, depression or even hopelessness. If so, you are not alone. As Christians I think many of us are under the false impression that when tough times come, we will not have to face all of the emotional and physical difficulties that are a part of life. God does deliver us from more things than we will probably ever know, but in most situations instead of delivering us from the situation Jesus is always faithful to be right there with us through all things and in all things.

When the prophet Jeremiah faced a difficult period in his life he wrote an amazing word of encouragement to which I have clung.

"I will never forget this awful time, as I grieve over my loss. Yet I still dare to hope when I remember this: The faithful love of the LORD never ends! His mercies never cease. Great is His faithfulness; his mercies begin afresh each morning." I say to myself, "The LORD is my inheritance therefore, I will hope in Him!"

-Lamentations 3:20-24 NIV

Perhaps you are facing an "awful" time in your life at this moment. As I write this, the tears are welling up in my eyes at the thought of the pain and uncertainty that you are facing. I may never meet you or know your name but you can be assured that I am praying to a Savior who does know your name and your situation and will always be faithful to His word.

Not a single one of us is exempt from the pain and uncertainties that life sometimes brings. Whether it is a loss of a job, the end of a relationship, a debilitating disease or the death of a loved one, all of us at some point in our life will face a situation that will test our faith and challenge our character.

Our faith may stand firm or it may waver under the load. Either way we all can be assured that Jesus will never leave us or forsake us (Hebrews 13:5).

No matter the diagnosis, prognosis or final result,

"The Lord will work out His plans for my life—for your faithful love, O Lord, endures forever."

-Psalm 138:8 NLT

Throughout the pages of this book you will join us on a journey that will encourage your spirit and strengthen your faith as you learn how Jesus proved Himself faithful time and time again. You will see how He went before us preparing many miracles before the need for them even happened.

We pray that our story will help reveal the minute and meticulous details that God organized in our story and is performing in your life at this very moment, details that can easily go unnoticed during the times in life when we struggle.

Our story has not ended and neither has yours. Our prayer is that throughout the pages of this book you will not only see the faithfulness of Jesus in our story but that it will bring a whole new revelation of His faithfulness into yours as well.

In 1 Corinthians 11:17-33 the Apostle Paul not only gives us instructions concerning the Lords Supper, but also tells us of the story of Jesus as He served the very first communion. In Paul's version, Jesus tells His disciples concerning the bread, "This is my body which was broken for you..."

Even though not a bone in his body was broken, thus fulfilling prophecy, Jesus was telling His disciples that He would die a broken man with a broken heart so that all of mankind could have healing and salvation through Him. **He is our Broken Healer.**

-Dan

Most people feel that life aimlessly wanders along until the end. Whatever comes comes. Some feel that God is very distant and uncaring. If He truly does care then why is He so often silent? In those times we wonder if He cares what happens in our life. We can easily get on that road of asking so many questions, even questioning our faith in God when life gets difficult.

The Holy Spirit reminded me of something while I was playing the "memory game" with my children. I have to say since I have had my kids, my relationship with God has gone to a new level, a new revelation of how He deals with, cares for and loves His children. Most of the time, I am taught by the Holy Spirit through my children and how I relate to them.

We were playing and, like me, my children play to win! Most of the time, we have real sorry losers in our house! Our game faces were on, but as we lifted each card and turned it over, something caught my attention. Without thinking I naturally knew where most of the matching pairs were, but was deliberately avoiding them so that my son or daughter would come after me and get them instead. No matter how long it took for Caelan and Rian to find them, I pretended that I didn't know or gave them subtle hints. I was amazed at how I wanted my children to win more than I wanted to, in everything, not just a simple card game, but in everything.

Instantly, the Holy Spirit spoke to me and said; "This is the very nature of God himself. For He has already won the game! He knows how to win! He is on your side. Even when it looks like you are going to lose, it's not over until the last card is played. Don't give up. Don't quit. He has it already thought out and put into plan – a Win! No one loses with GOD.

"If God is for us. who can be against us?"

-Romans 8:31 NLT

I was amazed at how that revelation was given to me and how it echoed through our life and the things we have written in this book. It is almost like you can see the winning cards being played by God in the hardest of circumstances. Of course,

I don't mean life is a game or God just gambles with our lives. But that He knows how to win because He has done it himself. He deliberately lets you win through Him cheering you on the whole way!

It recently occurred to me how God is always on time throughout the Bible. He put Queen Esther in the position to save her people. He gave Noah plans for the ark before it rained and flooded the land. No matter what our situation, God is there in the midst making a way for us.

Psalm 27: 5 (NLT) says, "For he will conceal me there when troubles come; he will hide me in his sanctuary, He will place me out of reach on a high rock."

We can choose whether or not to be obedient and go with God's plan. He still sets us up every day. He longs to see you win! I always knew this but it is amazing how we can know things for years yet we don't really understand them.

There is such a longing in a human heart to know that someone's looking out for us. When you watch the movies, the damsel in distress is always saved in the nick of time by her knight in shining armor. There's a running thread through our lives in which we long to have a rescuer or someone who is there with the right answer. We all long for that, right? You see the thing is, we do have that security or that rescuer in our lives and his name is Jesus Christ, but we seldom give Him a chance. Most times the cost seems too much and it asks so much of us, we feel it's just too hard so what's the point! To me it's kind of crazy to know that He knows all things, yet He is probably the last person we go to with life's problems. God knows how to do life well, keep Him in the front and continue to ask Him for His input and guidance daily into your life and He will make your path straight through the ups and downs of life!

"See, God has come to save me. I will trust in him and not be afraid. The Lord is my strength and my song; he has given me great victory".

-Isaiah 12: 2 NLT

-Miriam

Chapter 1

In the Beginning

You saw me before I was born. Every day of my life was recorded in your book. Every moment was laid out before a single day had passed.
- Psalm 139:16 NLT

Every story has a beginning. Ours, like yours, began with our parents. I know that I am stating the obvious, but without them there would not be any of us. The Bible tells us that before you and I were even conceived; God already knew us (Jeremiah 1:5), called us by our name (John 10:3) and had a plan and purpose for our lives (Jeremiah 1:5 & 29:11).

My story begins seven years before I was born in May of 1957. It was a beautiful southern California day and my parents, Harold and Joan, had just been maternity clothes shopping for my mom who was five months pregnant with her first child.

As they headed down the highway to the Christian book store they were filled with excitement, promise and song as they sang:

> "I don't know about tomorrow
> I just live from day to day
> And I don't borrow from its sunshine
> For its skies may turn to gray
> And I don't worry o'er the future
> For I know what Jesus said
> And today I'll walk beside Him
> For He knows what lies ahead
> Many things about tomorrow
> I don't seem to understand
> But I know who holds tomorrow
> And I know who holds my hand"[2]

At that moment, in mid song, as if God was preparing them for what was about to happen, a gasoline truck turned into their lane colliding with them head-on.

The collision was so violent that in the impact my dad's chest broke the steering wheel and knocked him unconscious. Miraculously, his injuries were minor.

As he regained consciousness, his first instinct was to check on the welfare of his wife. To his horror, her now limp body which only moments before had been full of hope and song, had been smashed against the windshield and the dashboard and now was slumped on the floorboard.

Those were the days long before seatbelts and the extent of her injuries would reflect that fact. The broken bone of her left femur sliced its way through her thigh and protruded out of her leg. The impact of her head against the windshield nearly removed her scalp and it would take 140 stitches to close her head wound.

In shock my father frantically tried to remove her limp body from the car. A gentleman on the scene pleaded with him to stop in fear that it might increase the severity of her injuries. He introduced himself as a Marine medic. As they waited the thirty agonizing minutes for the ambulance to arrive, the profuse bleeding from my mother's wounds had now flowed out of the car, into the street and ran down the gutter. At that point the medic applied pressure to her head wound which slowed the bleeding enough to keep her alive.

Across the street in a beauty shop a woman from my parents' church had witnessed the accident. Immediately after recognizing that it was my parents, she called their pastor, John R. Richie who in turn called the Bible College and the student body was mobilized to prayer.

At the hospital the doctors were preparing my father for the worst. They told him that due to the severity of the injuries they did not think she would survive and asked his permission to remove the five month old baby that was forming in her womb the moment she died. In the same breath he gave his consent and told them that hundreds of people were praying and she was going to survive. They responded the same way many doctors do who do not know the power of Jesus; they shrugged their shoulders and said, "I hope you are right."

In fear of her body regressing into deeper shock and instability, the doctors waited until the day after the accident to repair her head wound and waited two days before surgically repairing her leg.

My dad continually remained by her side waiting and praying that she would regain consciousness. After three days of unconsciousness suddenly he heard a quiet familiar voice say, "Where am I?"

I can hear the celebration and the shouts of, "Thank you Jesus!" fill that hospital room as if I were there. In reality, a part of me was there inside of her waiting for the day that my life would begin.

After three weeks in the hospital she was released to go home and my mother being my mother, began cooking and doing other household tasks while on crutches within a week of being discharged. On November 17, 1957 she gave birth to a seven pound three ounce healthy baby boy (Steven Harold Pope).

Before my father went through his graduation ceremony he waited for my mother to recover and return to school to earn her degree. It was a moment that they wanted to celebrate together: a moment that they thought would never become a reality only a few months before. Since then, they have ministered to thousands of people as pastors and as missionaries to Liberia in Africa. As we write this book they are still in ministry telling others the story of faithful Jesus.

Miracle in the Amazon

It was a bit of a shock for my mum to discover she was pregnant for the fourth time......not only because she already had three little girls, but we lived the middle of the Amazon

4

jungle! *The nearest hospital and medical help was 24 hours travelling time down the river in Manaus. Exactly what my parents should do about my birth was heavy on their hearts. The thought of packing up the whole family on an overcrowded river boat, not to mention finding accommodations, paying for a doctor and a hospital bed for a month caused them great anxiety. The alternative was staying at home in the jungle and asking a missionary colleague, Mary Blow, whether she was prepared to stay and deliver me in such an isolated place. Mary said yes and the decision was made to stay.*

Life was very difficult…..food was scarce. The menu everyday consisted of salted fish and rice. Not a great diet for a pregnant woman! They had no electricity and therefore water and light were a major problem.

In September 1978 my dad wrote in his prayer journal:

"Hot day…no electricity…town's generator is broken again. Had to fan Carol for several hours with a piece of cardboard! This day (September 14th) our lovely wee daughter, Miriam was born (not so wee, 8 pounds 12 ounces). For months we had difficulty with the electricity and water but the week that followed her birth was the most difficult, practically speaking, since coming to Brazil. We had no electricity which meant no light, no fridge and hardly any water. The river is rotten with the town's refuse. At the end of a hot day there was hardly a bucket of water to bath the whole household. We could not buy any gas for several weeks for cooking. Mary cared for her patient, the new baby and cooked for all the family on a small primus stove."

My birth was a miracle on so many levels. Mum said it was the best delivery of all five children! I arrived in 3 ½ hours in the dark, by torchlight (flashlight)! My early months were spent permanently under netting, protecting me from spiders, bugs and snakes.

A few months after my birth my whole family travelled down river by boat to Manaus to register my birth with the Brazilian and British authorities. Our neighbor was on the boat with his family taking his sick wife to Manaus. My dad found out later that she had hepatitis and of his family of eight, six had died of the disease.

Shortly after our return my mum became ill. She had a fever, nausea and had stopped eating. My parents assumed she had caught malaria but tests were negative. Within a week, my mum collapsed and was diagnosed with hepatitis. This was serious! She was very infectious and had to be isolated. Glucose drips hung on a nail over her bed as her emaciated seizure ridden body lay on what was thought to be her death bed.

Missionary colleagues found a Christian doctor, who after praying for her told everyone my mum was dying. In the midst of the uncertainty God gave my parents a promise to pray and stand on:

"I will <u>sustain</u> thee on thy sick bed and <u>heal</u> thee of thy infirmities."

- Psalm 41:3 KJV

That is precisely what God did! Slowly my mum began to recover. Not only did He sustain and heal but provided for every need. The doctor's comment on my mum's recovery was "Incredible"! When my dad received the bills for the medical attention and supplies, the doctor had cut my parents account by 2/3. They were left with the exact amount of money to pay off their remaining debts!

The doctor also gave my mum permission to travel. Our travel documents to return home to Northern Ireland, which had been delayed, were suddenly released. After the extreme difficulties of the previous five months, I arrived in Northern Ireland shivering in the cold but safe in my healed mum's arms.

"Know, recognize, and understand therefore that the Lord your God, He is God, the faithful God, Who keeps covenant and steadfast love and mercy with those who love Him and keep His commandments, to a thousand generations,"

- Deuteronomy 7:9 AMP

Chapter 2

From Northern Ireland with Love

Delight yourself also in the Lord, and He will give you the desires and secret petitions of your heart.

- Psalm 37:4 AMP

There are events in every generation for which you remember where you were and what you were doing when you heard the news. Do you remember what you were doing on December 31, 1999? Many around the world waited nervously to see if their computers would malfunction due to a computer glitch which many thought would shut down the modern world as we began a new century.

People needing to travel on airlines even cancelled their reservations in fear of what might happen. To my knowledge I do not remember one major problem, but I do remember praying a New Year's Eve prayer for my future wife, whoever she was. Little did I realize that six hours earlier Miriam had been standing on a bridge in

Belfast, Northern Ireland watching the fireworks light up the New Year's Eve sky.

In 2000, I completed my Bachelor of Arts degree in Fine Applied Arts (ceramics) from the University of Ulster in Belfast, Northern Ireland. Believe me, I was ready to have a break from clay and had agreed to and was very excited about being a part of a Youth Evangelism Team in America. I would be living in Ottumwa, Iowa along with three other young adults for one year.

I have to tell you that ever since I was a young girl I have always had a fascination with the United States, so it was a dream come true. When I first arrived my jaw dropped and my eyes were wide open in awe. Wow! There is a bus like in the movie Speed! There are the mailboxes that I've seen on TV! No way! You can even drive through at the bank. You Americans! I found it even stranger that someone bagged my groceries for me. The hardest thing for me is when my trolley (shopping cart) gets pushed out to my car and the groceries are unloaded by a stranger (grocery boy/girl)! What a nation of convenience.

That year was one of the most life-changing years that I have ever experienced. God completely transformed my relationship with Him and I have not been the same since.

In the previous year I had met another missionary from Northern Ireland who had been on the same one year mission's placement program.

Shane called and asked, "I have a friend named Barry on the current mission's team, would you go and introduce yourself to him?" I told Shane that I would be more than happy to.

On the morning of October 25th in 2000, as I was reading water meters (my job at that time) in the area where the mission's team was located, I thought I would do my duty and see if Barry was in. I knocked on the door and waited a few minutes and when no one came to the door, off I went. I had only driven a few blocks when the Holy Spirit began to speak to me and encourage me that I needed to go back. At first I must confess that I ignored what He was telling me. But the further I drove the stronger the message became to the point where I started to tremble. I turned my truck around and headed back to the YET (Youth Evangelism Team) house.

As I pulled up to the house I noticed there was a young lady sitting in a car in the driveway reading her Bible. I walked to the car and tapped on the side window, which of course startled her. She rolled down the window just an about an inch and then I introduced myself. "Hi I'm Dan Pope. I'm looking for Barry."

To my surprise she said, "I've heard of you."

So here I am trying to have my quiet time with the Lord. (Yes, in a car! It was hard to get time by yourself in a household of 4 other young adults). I was in my pajamas, morning breath, eye crusts, crazy hair, the whole works. The ironic thing is that I had prayed for years that my future husband would see me at my worst, so I could wow him with my best. I was only reminded of this thought after we started dating because our first meeting was definitely not love at first sight.

I wondered what this strange man was doing poking around our house so early in the morning (but he was actually reading meters). I was very suspicious of him and of course, he startled me so I was on my guard. I let him say what he wanted, closed the window and never thought of him again until several weeks later.

At that time I was the youth pastor of a thriving on fire for God youth group and with that came some negative (and a lot of positive) feedback from several of the churches in town. By the tone of her voice and her reaction when she said, "I've heard of you." I knew it wasn't a positive thing that she had heard.

I then blurted out, "Don't worry you're safe, I've already made my human sacrifice for the month."

Not the smoothest of opening lines, I know. As I walked away I remember thinking of how beautiful she was, not realizing that God had just introduced me to my future wife. As we began to get to know each other we were amazed how the first five years of our lives were so alike growing up in the jungles, Miriam in Brazil and me in Liberia, Africa. The rest is history as the saying goes.

I was thirty-six at the time and had pretty much given up on finding a helpmate for my life, but faithful Jesus hearing my prayer year after year came through in His time. I wrote this poem based on scripture and read it to Miriam the night we were engaged (in a surprise engagement skit in front of the entire church during a Sunday service).

<u>True Love</u>

The Spirit of the Sovereign Lord is upon us
Because He has anointed us
Alone, a thousand will fall at your side
Together, ten thousand will fall at our right hand
God said it is not good for man to be alone
So he created for him a wife so that he would be
complete

And the two shall become one in body, soul and
spirit
A wife of noble character is worth more than fine
jewels
Her husband has full confidence in her
And lacks nothing of value
I will sing your praises and call you blessed
I will love you as Christ loved the church and gave
Himself up for her
I will enjoy life with you as my wife, whom I love
Our love will soar on wings of eagles
Let me kiss you with the kisses of my mouth
For your love is more delightful than wine
Pleasing is the fragrance of your perfume
Your name is like perfume poured out
No wonder I love you
I rejoice and delight in you
My lover is mine and I am hers
For two are better than one
If one falls down, the other can help them up
If two lie down together, they will keep warm
Though one may be overpowered,
Two can defend themselves
A cord of three strands cannot be quickly broken
What the Lord has joined together-no one can
separate
And as for me and my house
We will serve the Lord
Together...forever.

During that first year in Iowa, I fell in love with America and the American people and one in particular, Pastor Daniel Pope. I have to laugh because after all of those years of looking, wondering and searching in Northern Ireland, God had to bring me to America to meet my future husband. It really made me realize that God knows your deepest desires.

In two months we were engaged and seven months after that we were married. My mum and dad never met Dan until a week before the wedding, so they had to really trust my decision. My poor mum basically was left to plan a wedding in Northern Ireland in a matter of months. We had two weddings, one in Northern Ireland and one in Iowa two weeks apart. It was a great experience but exhausting. We were so looking forward to our honeymoon.

That though was just the beginning of seeing faithful Jesus in action. What we have discovered in the years that followed is that Jesus isn't just faithful in the good times, but He has also proven Himself faithful in the most difficult of times. Up to that point we had a fairytale romance but the honeymoon was about to test the "for better or for worse" and the "in sickness and in health" part of our wedding vows.

Chapter 3

Rescued in the Rockies

"My thoughts are nothing like your thoughts,"
says the LORD. "And my ways are far beyond
anything -you could imagine."
-Isaiah 55:8 NLT

JUST MARRIED! What exciting words to see painted on the windows of your car! When you have two weddings on two continents in a matter of two weeks you can't wait to have time for yourselves as husband and wife. Bring on the honeymoon!

Dan had booked a beautiful and very romantic log cabin in Estes Park, Colorado, somewhere I had always wanted to go. The cabin was fully furnished with a king-size bed, hot tub in front of an open fire and the most breathtaking view of the Rocky Mountains. I had dreamt of this moment my whole young life and it was finally here. I was so excited and overjoyed at what God had given us. Alone, just the two of us, that is until a co-worker (Phil Carlo) told Dan that he and his wife (Carol) would be camping in Estes Park the same week that we would be there.

"Ok." I thought, but what are the chances we would actually run into them?

Then Phil dropped the bombshell that I was not expecting, "So give me your cell phone number and Carol and I will take you two newlyweds out to eat one night."

I had known Phil and Carol Carlo since moving to Ottumwa eight years earlier, and their daughter was part of our youth group. They are absolutely amazing people and only wanted to help us celebrate, but this was our honeymoon and we just wanted to be alone. What we didn't realize was that even before we had left on our honeymoon, faithful Jesus was putting into place the right people in the right place at exactly the right time to help us in a great time of need. **He was setting us up for a miracle.**

We were full of excitement and anticipation as we packed our small car. Finally we were on the road. I had to drive the whole way there because Miriam had never driven before, not even in Northern Ireland. She needed a social security number to get her learners permit and since she had just applied for her permanent residency, she was waiting for one to be issued. She wasn't used to such a long drive either due to the fact that you can fit Northern Ireland three times into Iowa, but we were so taken up with each other that the fifteen hour drive didn't matter at all.

On our second day of travel I began to get a severe headache but figured it was exhaustion and stress from the whirlwind weddings and the nonstop schedule we had just been through. I took some ibuprofen, which only seemed to help a little bit, and thought that once we had a chance to relax and rest I would feel fine.

As we began our final drive through the Big Thompson Canon with its sheer cliffs on either side of highway 34, I was telling Miriam that I remembered as an eleven year old hearing of the flash flood that took one hundred and forty-five lives on July 31, 1976 on this very stretch of road that we were now driving along. That thought soon faded as we gazed at the beauty that surrounded us.

We checked into our cabin and were amazed at the how perfect it was. After unloading the car we decided to drive into Estes Park and see the shops and find the restaurants. By this time my headache had increased to the point that I could barely function, but I was not going to let a headache ruin our honeymoon.

After spending several hours in town we went and had dinner. As I sat and ate my trout almandine (I always remember a great meal) I tried not to let on to Miriam just how sick I was feeling. After arriving at the cabin I thought a nice relaxing sit in the hot tub would help alleviate the thumping pain in my head... boy was I wrong! At this point all I wanted to do was go to sleep.

After a night of restless sleep my headache seemed to be a little better in the morning so we decided to drive up the Old Fall River Road to the Alpine Visitors Center. If you have never driven on the Old River Road, it is a very beautiful, windy, narrow eleven miles long, one way dirt road with steep drop offs that leads to an elevation of 11,796 feet and back onto highway 34. The drive would be no problem on a normal day but today was anything but normal.

As we began the ascent from Estes Park the severity of my headache began to intensify once again. This time I felt disoriented and dizzy, not a good combination when you are driving on such a challenging road. At one point I looked out my side window and noticed that I was driving on the edge of the road and all I could see were boulders twenty feet below. I eased the car back to the center of the road and thought that there was no way I should be driving on such a road. By this time we were half way up the mountain and even if I had wanted to head back down, I was on a one way road with only one option - finish the drive. When we arrived at the top of the mountain I was overwhelmed with relief.

When we arrived back in Estes Park, Miriam mentioned that she thought she might need to see a doctor about a medical issue that she was having. To our surprise the first doctor's office we called could see her right away, so off we went. As we were in the exam room I mentioned to the doctor that I had been having severe headaches so he looked me over and said all that he could see was a sinus infection and prescribed a course of antibiotics for the both of us.

Minutes later my cell phone rang.

"Hi Dan... Phil Carlo. Carol and I would like to take you and Miriam out to dinner tonight if you are free."

I had completely forgotten that the Carlos were in town that week. We accepted their invitation even though I was now experiencing a new symptom - nausea.

We met at lovely restaurant close to where the Carlos were camping. We talked, laughed and ate (fresh trout once again). At the end of the meal Phil said that he would like to show us their camp site, so we got in our car and followed them up a mountain road to the place where their camper sat. After a few minutes of small talk I told Phil I would see him at work next week and off we went. As we pulled away we talked about what nice people Phil and Carol were and how we enjoyed our night with them.

The next morning we decided to stay in town and just visit the shops since we both were not feeling well. As we went from one quaint shop to the next I found that each time I stepped back outside from the dimly lit shops, the light from the sun not only increased my headache but bothered my eyes to the point that I kept them open just enough to see where I was walking. As we stepped into a glass shop and began to watch a beautiful glass vase being blown, I suddenly became very dizzy, disoriented and nauseous.

As I quickly headed out the door I turned to Miriam and said, "I think I'm going to be sick."

Once outside I told Miriam that I needed to go back to the cabin and lie down for awhile before we continued our day.

I had just drifted off to sleep when I abruptly awoke, ran to the bathroom and spent the next two hours vomiting with such intensity that I began to vomit blood. It was at that point I told Miriam that she would have to drive me to the hospital. There were two problems: Miriam had never gotten a drivers license so she had zero driving experience and we had no idea where the hospital was.

So you need to know that I am not the best person to be helping out in this sort of situation. My gifting is definitely not a doctor, surgeon, nurse or first responder (I am an artist, a very emotional artist). If our children (or I) are sick it is Dan who takes care of us. So there I was battling nausea because he was sick. I have been known to break out in hives before exams, turn beet red and blotchy all over when speaking to people and develop a nasty, itchy skin condition when under serious stress.

Then on top of that he tells me that I have to take him to the hospital! Panic struck and my heart felt like it was coming out of my chest. I didn't have much time to think about it because he really needed medical attention. Thoughts of being stopped by the police and getting deported filled my head.

I just started to pray, "Oh, Lord please let there be no policemen around, please! Just get us there safe!"

I grabbed a plastic bag for him and helped him into the car, took a deep breath and started the engine. For those of you who have never been to the United Kingdom and Ireland, we drive on the other side of the road and our steering wheels are on the other side of the car. It was a challenge for me to even drive the car let alone be on the other side of the road. Of course, I hadn't a clue where we were going either. The roads were very hilly and windy, quite like back home in Northern Ireland (which didn't help because I had never driven there either). I had to keep asking Dan what to do and where to turn. Was I on the right side of the road? Poor soul, he was trying to keep his head low because when he sat upright he would get sick. I was in total hysterics. My whole body sighed with relief when we drove into the parking lot of the hospital. Little did I realize at that moment that there would be more adventures ahead!

I was taken to an exam room where the medical staff ran a number of tests on me which included drawing blood (I am not a fan of needles). They diagnosed me with altitude sickness and dehydration and said that after I received some oxygen and IV fluids I should feel dramatically better.

When the nurse returned with the IV I could tell that she was nervous. I use humor to cope with uncomfortable situations and chuckling nervously I said, "You look more scared than me."

My veins have always been difficult to find whenever I've needed blood drawn or an IV so I knew being so dehydrated wouldn't help matters any. After five or six attempts to find my vein including trying to corkscrew the IV catheter into my arm the nurse turned to me and said,

"I've only done this a few times before."

I suggested that she go get her supervisor and off she went. When they returned her supervisor took a look at me and said to the young nurse, "You're going to have to learn on someone so it might as well be him."

After three or four more attempts and me screaming like a toddler, the IV was finally in place.

After two hours of treatment, two IV's and a prescription for Demerol I was discharged and told to stay well hydrated.

As we drove back to the cabin, there thirty yards off the side of the road were several beautiful elk grazing. I have no idea what I was thinking at that moment, perhaps I had watched too many wild life shows but I asked Miriam to get out of the car and see if she could get a close up picture. She seriously wanted to hit me!

"A picture! Are you serious?" She said with a stern look and insisted that we go straight back to the cabin to rest. She had had enough stress that day to last her for the rest of her life. I kept on pleading with her and feeling bad for me, she told me she would get the picture.

Here I was sitting in the safety of the car and there she was literally climbing down into the ditch and sneaking up on the elk to get the picture. What a woman! It didn't even dawn on us until after she got back into the car just how dangerous her little adventure was. We look back at that moment now and laugh.

When we got back to the cabin I climbed into bed and drifted off to sleep totally exhausted. I had only been asleep for a few restless hours when the headache and nausea came storming back with a vengeance. I jumped out of bed and ran into the now familiar bathroom and began vomiting once again. This time it was more violent than before and the headache was so severe that I began screaming uncontrollably. It was now nine o'clock at night and Miriam would have to drive back to the hospital in the dark and without my help as I couldn't even lift my head off my lap as I sat in the car.

When we arrived at the emergency room there was a whole new staff on duty and I don't know what I looked like as I staggered up to the registration desk but immediately they notified the on call doctor. We informed the nurse that we had just been there six hours earlier and had been given a diagnosis of altitude sickness, had blood drawn and had been given two IV's before being discharged.

As the doctor looked over the records from my earlier visit he couldn't find the results from my blood test and called the laboratory to see if the results were there. Somehow my blood sample never made it to the lab because if it had I would have never been allowed to leave the hospital earlier that day. A second blood test revealed that my white blood count was highly elevated indicating a severe infection and all of my other symptoms were consistent with those of meningitis.

To confirm this diagnosis the doctor needed to perform a lumbar puncture so that my spinal fluid could be tested. As I sat up and leaned forward, rolling my back into position I kept repeating, "I want to be in a dark room. The lights are making it worse!" The muscles in my back had become so tense and rigid by this time that after three failed attempts causing a hematoma the procedure was aborted. I was then administered Rocephin which is a medication used to treat life threatening bacterial infections.

We were then informed that I would need to be transferred to Poudre Valley Hospital in Fort Collins, Colorado for further treatment.

When the doctor told me that they were going to transfer Dan, it took every ounce of strength in me to keep my composure. Then he added at the end of the conversation that I couldn't ride with him due to some sort of rule. The doctor asked if I had a car and I said, "Yes (gulp)."

He told me to just follow the ambulance to Fort Collins. I was smiling and nodding my head but inside I was freaking out thinking, "No, you can't do that to me! How am going to get there? I can't do that, seriously!"

By this time, Dan was completely drugged. He couldn't hold a conversation at all. I was completely alone and so scared. I didn't know what to do! Dan was always the one who dealt with problems and knew the answers. We had only been in our beautiful cabin a few days and I would have to go back and pack everything, tell the hotel what happened, check out, (which I didn't even know how to do) and go to the other hospital (which I didn't know how to get to).

I started frantically praying, "Lord, please, help me! What I am going to do?"

Just before they wheeled Dan out of the room and into the ambulance he whispered, "Go get Phil."

I had totally forgotten about the Carlos being in Estes Park. At that moment, it felt like a good idea, then I realized that it was 2 a.m., pitch black outside and didn't know how to get to their campsite from the hospital.

I left the Hospital in total shock about what the situation was requiring me to do. I heard myself say continually, "You have to do this you have no choice!"

Oh, my word, I was an alien who had just applied for legal residency and was now driving illegally in the dark with no map and no clue where I was going. I look back at that night and don't know whether I would even do it now (I have now been legally driving in the U.S for 10 years). I got into the car, took a deep breath and drove out of the parking lot.

One of our very good friends, Barb, had told me, "When you are driving on the road, right is right!" I was speaking that out all the way to the campsite (thanks Barb). I don't remember much about getting there. I can honesty tell you that it was only by the grace of God and the Holy Spirit reminding me of the drive just the day before that got me there. I am absolutely terrible with directions; seriously, I couldn't believe I had made it there. That was just as much of a miracle to me as the parting the Red Sea!

I felt bad knocking on the window of the Carlo's camper so late, but I needing someone to help me. After several attempts at knocking, a half asleep Phil pulled back the curtain and peered out the window. Rubbing his eyes he said, "Yes?"

Frantically I told him what had happened and that I was so sorry for bothering them but I had no one else to turn to.

In no time at all, they were dressed and came out of their camper. Phil asked where they took him and I told him Fort Collins. He didn't know how to get there but that didn't stop him. The three of us got in the car and started on our way. No map. No directions. He just tried to find his way there. Something I could never do. I remember just sitting in the back seat of the car saying, "Lord, Please get us there....let us not be going in the opposite direction".

We had been driving for over an hour through the winding mountain roads when I heard Phil say, "We're here."

I felt like crying. What a relief, faithful Jesus had gone before us and placed the Carlos in the center of our honeymoon to be our rescuers in the Rockies.

Chapter 4

Honeymoon in the Hospital

He will cover you with his feathers.
He will shelter you with his wings.
His faithful promises are your armor and protection.
-Psalm 91:4 NLT

Have you ever ridden in an ambulance a long distance? If you haven't, let me assure you that they are definitely not built for comfort especially on a narrow winding mountain road.

The first few hours at the Poudre Valley Hospital I felt all alone, wondering if Miriam was safe and was she able to find the Carlos. All else was a blur of bright lights, faces, pokes and prods.

After being reassessed by the emergency room doctor I was taken to a private room on the Neurological Unit and administered heavy doses of antibiotics and pain medication. As I drifted off to sleep I prayed, "Lord, please help Miriam and keep her safe."

The honeymoon of her dreams had now turned into a nightmare.

I was awakened a few hours later by a very kind nurse who informed me that he was there to wheel me down to x-ray for a CT scan. All I remember about our conversation was him asking me where I was from and what was I doing in Colorado. His caring demeanor helped calm my fears.

I must have been quite a sight because as I sat in the waiting area in a wheelchair my head nodding and my eyes barely open because of the pain the light caused, I noticed a man at the other end of the room staring at me. Minutes later I was then taken to the CT room where I fell asleep as the hum of the machine began.

I can't remember much about arriving at the hospital other than the Carlos walking me up to Dan's room. They asked me if they could take the car back to Estes Park and bring some refreshments for me the next day. I told them that would be fine and off they went. We are forever indebted for the kindness they showed us.

I was now in Dan's room, sitting by his bed holding his hand. He didn't know that I was even there (due to all the drugs) which upset me a lot especially after all that I had just been through. I just needed him at that moment, but he was unable to respond. I went into the bathroom, sobbed and fought off nausea and sickness due to all the emotion I had been feeling up to that moment.

A honeymoon is meant to be a very special time between a husband and wife. A time where the husband delights in his wife, but mine was unconscious in a hospital bed and not even able to notice that I was there. I know that it sounds very selfish but that's how I felt at that moment. I had dreamt about this moment for years; my wedding, my honeymoon and my happy-ever-after life. Isn't that what every girl wants? It felt as though in the past few hours, my preconceived dreams had been completely shattered. I still didn't know what was wrong with him or what had happened. As usual, my thoughts started going crazy...I had just married the love of my life and now I thought that I was about to lose him.

There was nothing we could do but wait. Wait for the fever to break, wait for the medications to work and wait for the word on when I would be discharged from the hospital.

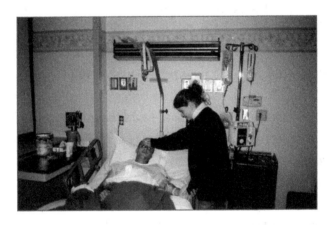

Miriam would climb into the small hospital bed with me and we would spend hours talking, watching TV and I would doze off to sleep as my body fought off the infection.

After a few days of being on the antibiotics the neurologist came into my room holding a tray that had a syringe with a very long needle on it. She informed me that, due to the failed lumbar puncture a few days earlier, she would have to attempt yet another one. After looking over my chart and thoroughly checking me from head to toe she commented, "For someone who has been diagnosed with meningitis, you sure are looking awfully well."

Then she spoke the words that made me much less nervous, "I don't think I am going to do the puncture since you are responding so well to treatment."

The honeymoon that we had meticulously planned was now relegated from a beautiful mountain cabin to a hospital room overlooking a parking lot. Instead of the king sized bed, hot tub and fireplace, I was in a hospital bed with an IV in my arm and Miriam had to sleep in a recliner chair next to my bed. It was not very romantic but at least we were together.

After several more days of treatment my conditions had improved to the point that the neurologist had decided to discharge me into the care of my family physician back in Iowa. With all of my medical records in tow, a prescription of antibiotics and pain medication, we were headed back home.

On the first day of travel Carol drove our car since I was still feeling very weak and tired. After eight hours on the road I desperately needed to climb into a bed and get some sleep so we stopped at a motel for the night. The next morning the Carlos needed to leave very early and wanting to get more rest, I assured them that I was capable of driving the rest of the way home, (much to Miriam's displeasure – she was furious that I would even attempt such a thing).

What we had thought was an intrusion into our honeymoon when Phil and Carol had told us that they too would be in Estes Park and that they wanted to take us out to dinner was really faithful Jesus preparing us for a miracle before we even knew there would be a need for one.

After returning home I went to see my doctor the very next day. I continued antibiotic treatments for four more weeks before the infection was completely gone. My physical strength eventually returned after two more weeks of rest but the hurt and disappointment of a ruined honeymoon lingered for much longer.

Oh, by-the-way, two years later I took Miriam to Florida for a wonderful second honeymoon and she was excited to see flat straight roads and even more excited that she didn't have to drive on them!

Chapter 5

Shattered

"Please, Lord, rescue me! Come quickly, Lord, and help me."
-Psalm 40:30 NLT

The next five years would be filled with the business of married life as a bi-vocational youth pastor. On July 24, 2003 we had a new addition as our beautiful and creative daughter, Caelan Joan Victoria was born. Two-and-a-half years later, on January 11, 2006 God blessed us with our handsome and intelligent son, Rian Gerald William.

During this time Miriam's brother, William, had been living with us for nearly a year and was in America on a religious workers visa helping minister at our church. We had hit it off the very first night that we had met in Northern Ireland the week that Miriam and I were married, so having him live with us was a joy. What none of us knew at the time was that God was once again going before us preparing the way for what was about to happen.

It was a mild afternoon on December 3, 2006 when we arrived home from church. I turned on the TV expecting to watch the Chicago Bears football game but to my disgust the channel that the game was on was not coming in clearly. We had recently signed up with a satellite company but for some reason our community would not allow local programming in the package. Our only option to receive local stations was the old fashioned way, a television antenna that was at the very peak of our roof.

It seemed easy enough; climb a ladder to the top of the roof, adjust the antenna and then sit back with Will and enjoy an afternoon of football. I put on my coat, grabbed my cell phone (so that I could call Miriam to see if the reception was improving as I adjusted the antenna) and out the door I went.

Okay, let's rewind the story slightly. Yes, we did just get home from church, which is a crazy time when you have small children who are very hungry and want their lunch. Dan put his coat on and I thought to myself, "Seriously, you're leaving, now?"

I asked where he was going and with a sheepish look he said, "You won't like where I am going".

I immediately knew where he was headed so I rolled my eyes and carried on dealing with the children. He then handed me the phone wanting me to tell him when the picture came in clear. Of course, I took the phone even though I was not impressed but I knew that he wanted to watch the game.

No matter what direction I moved the antenna; the reception wasn't getting any better. It was at that point that I decided to step over the peak of the roof from the south side of the house to the north side to see if I could get a better angle of adjustment on the antenna. What I didn't notice as I stepped over the peak was that the north side of the roof was a sheet of ice from the peak to the gutter. That is, until it was too late. Down I went with a thud, cell phone flying through the air.

We had been communicating back and forth for awhile and then I heard a weird sound. Something had just bounced on the roof several times almost like someone had thrown a stone on the roof. The phone went quiet so I called out, "Dan? DAN!"

But he didn't answer. We had a big window, overlooking our back yard so I went over to have a look to see if something had happened.

The only thing that had kept me from sliding the twenty feet to the edge of the roof and then free falling an additional thirteen feet to the ground was a shingle that I had managed to grab hold of when I fell. I tried to get some form of traction with my feet so that I could ease my way a few feet up the roof, grab onto the antenna and pull myself back onto the south side of the roof. As I struggled to gain traction what I didn't realize was that the shingle which was the only thing that was keeping me from plummeting to the ground was beginning to tear due to my movement and weight.

I stared at that shingle in disbelief as it completely tore loose. Everything seemed to move in slow motion and I was completely helpless to do anything but allow gravity to take effect. I began sliding down the forty-five degree angled roof on my stomach feet first gaining speed along the way as I frantically dug my fingernails into the ice trying to slow down. As I was nearing the edge of the house I heard what seemed to be an audible voice say, "Land on your feet!"

At that moment in one fluid motion I quickly flipped over onto my back, sat up and was instantly launched into the air.

Seconds after I got to the window, I saw Dan literally falling from the roof onto the frozen ground inches away from a bush.

That bush was ten feet away from the house. I was traveling at such a velocity that not only was I thrown that far but it also increased the impact at which I landed. As I landed feet first, it sounded like glass shattering as my legs crumpled beneath me. Instantly I grabbed them and began to scream in agony.

I knew it was bad and immediately called 911. He was groaning and crying so hard that the neighbors came out to see who was making all the noise. Rian was sleeping at the time and Caelan kept asking me what that sound was. I turned the volume on the TV up loudly to keep her entertained and ran out to be by his side. I tried to calm him but nothing I said helped! I kept on saying, "They're coming. The ambulance is on its way."

The firefighters were the first on the scene and as they came around the corner of the house I could hear one of them say, "Oh, this is bad!"

Those are not the first words you want to hear from your rescuers. Minutes later the ambulance arrived.

After cutting off my clothes and checking me from head to toe, I could hear the paramedics and firefighters discussing the dilemma of how they were going to lift me onto the gurney. Due to the jellyfish like condition of my legs they were not able to transfer me by lifting my legs. After a few minutes of discussion they decided to use a two piece gurney called a "scoop board". Both pieces were carefully slid underneath me and then locked into place enabling the paramedics to transfer me onto the gurney and then into the ambulance.

As I was being wheeled down the driveway William and his fiancée (my niece) Bridget had just arrived back from picking up our lunch from Applebee's. I can still remember the look on their faces as I was wheeled past them.

I met them in the driveway and told them what had happened. William had helped out with the kids on numerous occasions so he knew their routines and what to do. I knew that they would be safe with him so that I could follow the ambulance to the hospital. This was a God moment for me; I didn't have family in America so having William live with us for nearly two years off and on was such a comfort for me. It would have been my worst nightmare to have had to drop the kids off with people they didn't know for who knows how long.

I then sat in our van behind the ambulance and waited. I had sat there for nearly twenty minutes wondering what was taking them so long to transfer Dan to the hospital. I called Dan's parents to inform them what had happened and continued to pray as I waited.

I had never felt such severe pain in all of my life. From the moment that I hit the ground the only time I stopped screaming in pain was long enough to answer the paramedic's questions. They were advised to begin an IV with morphine and the delay that Miriam was wondering about was due to the same problem the nurse had a few years earlier in Estes Park - the paramedics were having trouble getting the IV started. After each of the six failed attempts the paramedic would apologize. I remember telling him, 'That's okay; I've always been a hard stick."

When the morphine was finally administered I faded in and out of what seemed like a dream.

Once we arrived at the emergency room I stood by Dan's bed holding his hand as he faded in-and-out of consciousness, a scene that seemed all too familiar. I remember looking at his crushed foot and seeing that the side of it had been blown open due to the force of the impact and the shattering of the bones.

I don't think Dan knew the severity of his injuries at that point and all he kept saying was how stupid he was for climbing on the roof. I kept telling him that everything was going to be fine even though I had to leave the room several times to regain my composure.

I had not fully grasped how badly I was injured until the attending physician told us that I would need to be transferred immediately to either Mercy Hospital in Des Moines, Iowa or the University of Iowa Hospital in Iowa City. I asked the doctor if he were in my place which would he choose. Since the orthopedic department at the University of Iowa Hospital is considered one of the best in the nation, he said that would be his choice. In that case, Iowa City it was.

So here I am in nearly the same predicament as on our honeymoon. My husband is in the emergency room and now I find out that he needs to be transferred to a large hospital in a much bigger city. By this time I had become a legal resident and had had my driver's license for three years. I had no need to panic like I did in Estes Park or at least that was what I kept telling myself. I had experience driving around our small city but I had never driven outside of town especially in a much larger city. What was I going to do?

I called our pastor, Bill Hornback and told him what had happened. Without hesitation he told me that he would take me to Iowa City and stay as long as I needed him to. What a relief.

I then called Dan's mum and dad to let them know what I was going to do. They were already packed and ready to make the one hour drive from Bettendorf, Iowa to Iowa City. They told me that they had booked a motel room and that I was welcome to stay with them. As Pastor Bill and I made our way to the hospital in Iowa City he kept encouraging me to keep my thoughts positive. This was a drive that stirred up emotions not only about what was happening but what had happened years earlier on our honeymoon.

I was in a drug induced state of unconsciousness when I was loaded into the ambulance and remained that way until I was wheeled into the emergency room of the University hospital. For a brief moment it all seemed like a flashback to the Poudre Valley Hospital in Fort Collins, Colorado but the severe pain of my shattered legs quickly reminded me that this was not a dream.

Chapter 6

Waiting

But those who wait for the Lord [who expect, look for, and hope in Him] shall change and renew their strength and power; they shall lift their wings and mount up [close to God] as eagles [mount up to the sun]; they shall run and not be weary, they shall walk and not faint or become tired.

-Isaiah -40:31 AMP

So there I was in the ER waiting area at the University of Iowa Hospital along with Dan's mum, dad and our pastor. It seemed like the longest wait of my life. So many questions were running through my head wanting to be answered. All I kept on saying was "I can't believe this is happening to us again. What just happened?"

I have watched so many medical fiction and non-fiction programs on TV - exciting, heart-pounding, suspenseful dramas that unfold before your eyes leaving you feeling like you can't wait for next week to see what happens.

I wasn't feeling like that at this moment. Things weren't resolved in an hour like on those TV shows. I couldn't switch off this episode or fast forward it to see if it had a good ending, though I wished that I could have. Or better yet, rewind and stop it before it happened! Wouldn't it be nice to have a remote control in life? I felt that if someone had told me it was a joke, I would have believed them. But it wasn't, it was real and it was happening to us, once again.

After waiting for what seemed like an eternity we were finally allowed to see him. Walking down the corridor, the doctors and nurses were busily doing their jobs and family members of other patients randomly lined the walls. When we walked into his room, he was lying on a bed with weights stretching his legs so that they wouldn't collapse. His body was shaking so badly that I assumed he was in shock. His eyes were so piercing and he just kept apologizing over and over. I just held his hand and told him it was an accident.

Even though I like to watch hospital shows on television I am not a fan of the real thing. I think we all have been desensitized to what really happens in life! I had been fighting nausea since walking into the room and kept on telling myself, "Try and keep it together and try not to focus on what just happened." Whether or not that was the right thing to say to myself at the time I don't know, but it got me through it. I was relieved to see a young intern enter the room with information about Dan's condition.

I was fading in and out of consciousness to the voices and questions of the medical staff. When the weights and traction were placed on my legs I was amazed at how such a simple procedure could alleviate so much pressure and pain. While the doctor was adjusting the weights I turned and looked to my right and noticed that my parents, my pastor and my beautiful wife were standing in the room visibly upset.

When the orthopedic trauma surgeon arrived the burly, average height man bent over my gurney and said, "I'm Doctor Todd McKinley." He then assured me, "Even if you had been hit by a freight train I would be able to put you back together again."

I had still not been informed of the condition that I was in so I found that to be an odd introduction.

He then went on to tell me that my left tibia plateau (knee) had been shattered into forty pieces and my right calcaneous (heel) was one the worst crushed heels that he had ever seen and that one of my lumbar vertebrae was also fractured. The first words out of my mouth were, "Will I be able to go back to work?"

I worked as a meter reader for the Ottumwa Water and Hydro where I walked between six and ten miles a day. My only concern at that moment was wondering if I would be able to provide for my family.

The next words out of the surgeon's mouth were ones that I did not expect to hear, "With the severity of your injuries I can't guarantee that you will ever walk again."

For the first time I understood the seriousness of my condition.

He then continued, "If you are able to walk again, you will be very limited in what you will be able to do"

Even though that was such a grave prognosis, at that very moment I had a deep peace in my heart as if the Holy Spirit, the Comforter, as Jesus calls Him, was caressing my head with His hand like so many of us have done to comfort our children while He assured me that everything was going to be okay.

Doctor McKinley then informed me that due to the swelling of my legs, the reconstructive surgery I would need could not be performed until the swelling subsided. However, I would still need to have a cast placed on my right leg and foot and due to the extreme damage to my left leg and knee I would need to have an operation first thing in the morning to place an external fixator on my leg so that it would be properly supported.

It was the early hours of the morning when Joan, Harold and I arrived at the hotel after being at the hospital. There wasn't much conversation between us; I think we were all in a state of shock! I continually thought that if I could just sleep when I woke up everything would be back to normal. But I had this eerie feeling that I couldn't shake off, one that sits in the pit of your stomach. Would he make it through the night? Surgery was at 6 a.m. so we all went to bed trying to rest for a few hours before returning to the hospital. I tossed and turned most of the night, wondering if the kids were ok – Were they crying for me? I hoped they would sleep through the night for William. What kind of future was before us all? I think we all felt that we really didn't know what the morning would bring but we just had to leave it all in God's hands. After all He is the one who gives and takes away.

Normally this procedure would not take as long as other surgeries. It involved aligning my leg into its proper position then screwing two six inch titanium screws through my thigh and into my femur and then two more six inch screws just above my ankle. After those were in place a series of rods and locked hinges were attached to the screws making my knee completely immobile.

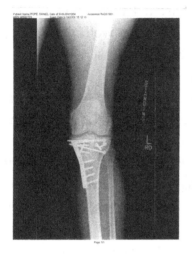
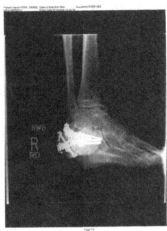

I don't remember being wheeled into the operating room; my next memories were of a young man and woman hurriedly pushing my gurney down a hallway as I stared at the ceiling lights racing past. I kept trying to sit up, not realizing where I was and without missing a step, one of them in a calm voice touched my shoulder and told me that I needed to remain still. I then looked down and for the first time noticed the unfamiliar contraption on my leg. I quickly faded into unconsciousness.

Suddenly I sat up as if awakened from a nightmare to the sound of the same whirring noise I had heard in Fort Collins. Quickly the radiologist assured me that it was okay and that I needed to lie back down so that they could get an accurate CT scan image of my chest. I still had no idea where I was or what was happening to me but I could tell by the tension on their faces and in their voices that this was a serious matter. I then faded back into unconsciousness.

Meanwhile, I had been waiting with Dan's parents and Pastor Bill for approximately eight hours and had not been given an update on what was happening. There was a specific waiting room that we were supposed to go to and wait while Dan was having surgery, but unfortunately we were never told this and unbeknownst to us we were not only waiting in the wrong room but were also on the wrong floor. Because of this the surgeon had no way of knowing where we were to give us an update.

As the hours went past, the unknown turned into panic. Dan's dad, Harold, continually demanded information from the nurses' station but being in the wrong waiting room, the nurses had no information to give. It was early afternoon when the surgeon finally showed up, very apologetic about the mix-up. I was so desperate to hear any news at all that I quickly forgot about the wait altogether. He told us that the surgery had gone well but Dan's injuries were very severe and he couldn't guarantee if he would be able to walk again. He said "Some people walk out of here and some don't".

I don't think those words really registered at that moment. It was almost as if my mind was ignoring the reality of the situation. Later that day, we were finally able to see him. I found it extremely difficult to look at Dan in that condition. He was very pale and his entire body was swollen and bruised. Afterwards, I spoke to a lady from our church that had gone up to visit Dan a few days after the accident. She said she was so upset at seeing him that she had to leave the room so that she could compose herself. Her words were "It just didn't look like him." He was in a lot of pain and not very responsive in those early days. We were so grateful for all the worldwide prayer, thoughts and support that we were receiving at that moment.

We had still not heard the reason why we had to wait for such a long time to get information about what was happening with Dan. The surgeon's delay was due to us not being in the right waiting room, but after Dan had been wheeled into the post operative recovery room he had no idea of what had transpired after the surgery. It wasn't until a few hours later that we heard the rest of the story, a story that if I had known it while we were waiting and wondering, it would have pushed me emotionally over the edge.

Through difficult times you don't always have a deep sense of the Holy Spirit at work but yet He is. Most times we ask a lot of questions – Where are you Lord? Can you even hear me? But through the later events that just happened in our story, I felt a continuous inner peace and acceptance. A week after the accident, I spoke at our home church. Dan lead a night called "Saturate" every Sunday night. It was a night a deep intimate worship with some scripture God had put on our hearts to speak the week before. I truly don't know how I ever did it! I only knew it was the word that needed to be spoken. I shared a message that the Holy Spirit gave to me days after the accident, about the church being a "Broken Body". God was longing to fix, reset and restore the Body, so it could do the same for others. This is the picture that was revealed to me:

We were all broken but no one seemed to be fixed. There were people there who had fresh wounds and people there who had been broken so long that it then healed that way. All of the people were hobbling, crawling and lying with broken arms, legs, hands or feet. Something didn't work right on their bodies.

I could see them trying to help each other; they weren't trying to help themselves as you normally see people with injuries do. But there were trying to hold each other, pull each other up from the ground etc. They couldn't do what they wanted due to their own injuries. Some injuries caused a lot of pain when they tried to move. Everyone was walking around totally incapacitated.

Suddenly, I felt the Holy Spirit start to explain the picture that I had just seen. I felt Him say:

"Yes, you are ALL broken, unable to do what the Body has been called to do! You want to help others but you are worse off than some of the ones you want to help. Therefore, you are unable and cause more damage to yourself and others! You cannot complete the purpose that God has called you to until you let Him fix you! He needs to heal you, restore you, and also reset you! This means He will have to re-break those areas which are already set wrong. It is impossible for you to help anyone until you yourself have been healed."

Psalm 147:3 (NLT) tells us, "He heals the brokenhearted and bandages all their wounds."

Since then, I have had a deep longing to see the Body rise up to what it is called to be. I long for the Body "individually" to totally surrender to the only One who can correct any "defects in our walk as a church body" and stimulate growth and true love for each other. To confidently walk in Jesus' footsteps, so the world truly knows He really does live! I urge the body to lift itself up to the Broken Healer! The One who knows how to restore, heal and unify His church so we can start to show His unconditional love and power in this difficult world in which we live in.

Chapter 7

On the Edge of Eternity

He alone is my rock and my salvation,
my fortress where I will not be shaken.

-Psalms 62:6 NLT

You know that God has performed a miracle when a hematologist stands at the side of your bed with a smile on his face and says, "You are a very lucky man, not very many people who have such a large pulmonary embolism live through the episode."

The words instantly came out of my mouth, "You mean I should have died?"

Doctor Rose is one of the kindest caring doctors that I had ever encountered and whenever he passed Miriam in the hall he would always call her by her name when enquiring how she was doing. He went on to explain to us the events that had taken place just a few hours before.

He told us in great detail that while I was in the recovery room after the operation, my heart went into tachycardia and my vital signs began to plummet. It was at that point that I was rushed to radiology to have a CT scan taken of my chest. The scan revealed a large pulmonary embolism.

He went on to tell me that a large blood clot had formed in my shattered left leg and that it had dislodged during the operation and made its way into my heart. At that moment my heart began to race as it forced the clot through the right ventricle and into the pulmonary artery where it made its way to the entrance of my right lung. Due to the size of the blood clot the doctor went on to say that it should have been impossible for the blood to flow past the clot and into my lung.

My response was, "It might be a medical impossibility but with God, all things are possible."

He smiled and said, "Someone is definitely watching over you."

He informed us that I would be staying on the trauma unit for at least a week where I would be closely monitored and that I would also need to be on blood thinners for at least six months. If all went well the blood clot would dissolve. Doctor Rose then went on to tell us that there was always the chance of the clot dislodging and moving further into my lung and there was also the possibility of other blood clots forming.

I immediately began receiving a daily shot of Levenox in my abdomen. I must confess that I am terribly phobic of needles so the thought of a shot in my abdomen was very disconcerting. Then when the nurse told me that I would be administering my own shots so that when I was finally released to go home I would be able to inject myself that was more than I thought I could handle. When I saw I had no choice, there I was, syringe in hand, needle against my skin waiting...finally I mustered up enough courage and stuck myself and pushed down the plunger. To my surprise it wasn't as bad as I expected it to be. I not only had I to deal with daily sticks but my blood needed checked on a daily basis at first and then weekly for the next seven months. Not what a person with a fear of needles looks forward to.

When the doctor left the room I wept violently.

The Bible tells us in Psalm 56:8, "You keep track of all my sorrows. You have collected all my tears in your bottle. You have recorded each one in your book."

I don't know how many tears I cried over the nearly one year of recovery, but my bottle must be the size of an ocean and there must be volumes of books detailing each one. I don't think that I was crying because one more thing had been added to the list of physical obstacles that needed to be overcome or because the thought that I was so close to death. I was crying at the realization that Miriam had been so close to being a widow and Caelan and Rian had been so close to being without their father.

How many tears have you shed over the pain and uncertainty that life has brought? How many times have you felt so all alone and afraid wondering if anyone truly understands what you are facing? How many questions have you asked, only to hear silence?

One question that I have asked many times is, "Why did I live and others die?" Why did a cousin of mine die of leukemia, leaving a devastated husband and three children behind? How difficult must it be for our friends who lost a child and constantly wonder what he would look like as he grew up? Why did a family in our home church just have to say good-bye to their 20 year old daughter who within months after its discovery lost her battle with leukemia? These and many others constantly carry the scars and endlessly ask the question, "Why?"

I wish that I had the answers for them. I wish that I knew why God chooses to spare one person's life while He takes others to their eternal home with Him. At times I found myself struggling with guilt at the fact that I did live. The only answer that I have is that God has numbered the days of my life and yours (Psalms 139:16) and not even the certainty of death due to a pulmonary embolism could cut my life a day shorter than He had planned for. It is comforting to know that our lives are in the hands of the Creator of all things and no matter what the doctors tell us or what the circumstances look like, it is God who determines life and death. Even in death, we who have Jesus as our Savior have new life to look forward to in His presence.

Paul tells us in 2 Corinthians 5:1-4 (NLT),

"For we know that when this earthly tent we live in is taken down (that is, when we die and leave this earthly body), we will have a house in heaven, an eternal body made for us by God himself and not by human hands. We grow weary in our present bodies, and we long to put on our heavenly bodies like new clothing. For we will put on heavenly bodies; we will not be spirits without bodies. While we live in these earthly bodies, we groan and sigh, but it's not that we want to die and get rid of these bodies that clothe us. Rather, we want to put on our new bodies so that these dying bodies will be swallowed up by life."

Six months after my pulmonary embolism was discovered, I was back at the hematology department at the University of Iowa Hospital for a follow-up appointment, this time with the head of the department. He sat down looked at me and repeated what I had heard six months earlier, "It is a miracle that you are alive."

He went on to inform me that I would be on the blood thinners for another month and then he would discontinue the treatments. I was then told that I needed to watch closely for any signs of another blood clot in my leg or in my lung.

I have had a few scares in the years that have followed but again faithful Jesus has been walking with me, just as His Word says. I may not be able to run and jump the way that I used to and I may have to deal with chronic pain at this moment, but I know without a doubt that one day I will be completely healed, either in this life or the next and so will you.

There are still times that I reflect on that moment of teetering on the edge of eternity. I find myself having mixed emotions as my spirit longs to be in heaven but my flesh longs to be with my wife and children.

Chapter 8

In the Still of the Night

Be still and know that I am God.
-Psalm 46:10 NLT

I hated the nights. If you have ever been in the hospital especially long term, perhaps you felt that way too.

During the first few nights after the accident I was terrified to go to sleep because every time I did I was tormented by nightmares. I would have the same dreams over and over again.

In one of the dreams, I would dream of falling off the roof and as I was in mid air my legs were torn off my body, landing on the ground with me falling on top of them. As this dream was repeated over and over again every time my legs were torn off they would land on top of each other until the pile of legs reached to the top of the roof.

In the second dream (at least I think it was a dream) I would see hideous demonic creatures grabbing and tearing at my flesh like hungry animals trying to drag me into a grave with my flesh and blood splattering all that was near. I would wake up trembling, in a panic and drenched with sweat.

No wonder I hated the nights.

It was during one of those moments when I was awakened by a nightmare that the Holy Spirit brought the story of Job to my mind. My experience wasn't even close to what Job had faced. His children were killed by a natural disaster as they celebrated one of their birthdays; he lost all of his livestock and most of his wealth; he was struck with disease and was left with a nagging wife who told him to curse God and die. Yet in all of this pain and uncertainty he fell on his face and worshipped God.

So there I was, tormented by nightmares, delirious with pain, terrified at my circumstances and while the tears streamed down my face soaking my pillow, I began to worship God with every fiber of my being. At that moment I found myself closer to God than I had ever been. I was discovering that God is truly close to the broken hearted (Psalm 34:18).

As the nightmares faded the fear was replaced by insomnia. After my family and friends had left for the evening and there were no more distractions I was forced to face the reality that I was confined to a bed in which I could only lie in one position, flat on my back. My legs had to be propped up on a pile of pillows to help alleviate the swelling and this contributed to even more discomfort. I would raise and lower my bed just to get the sensation of movement.

I could hear the muffled sounds of conversations coming from the nurses' station and the sound of call buttons going off throughout the night. There were so many times in between the two hours that my vitals were checked that I wanted to push my button just so that I would have someone there to talk to so that my mind wouldn't be consumed with the fear and uncertainty of my condition.

I don't really know what it was about the night. I would lie there awake and wonder what life was like at home. It was just a few weeks before Christmas and I so longed to be there watching the holiday cartoons with the kids next to me on the couch. I would wonder if I would ever again be able to chase Caelan and Rian around the yard or go on walks with Miriam. I would lie there and weep as I missed my wife and children terribly.

The still of the night would always seem to bring out all the fear and anxiety of my situation. I would lie there and wonder what my life would be like if I was unable to walk again or if the blood clot had ended my life, leaving Miriam and the kids to cope with the loss?

I don't know how many times I turned the channels on the TV each night but I'm sure over the two months that I spent in the hospital it must have been at least a thousand times. I needed something to distract me while I fell asleep.

When the nurses came in to check on me during the night I would try and keep them in my room as long as possible by chatting about anything I could think of. They were always so gracious and understanding and unless they were swamped by their duties they would always take the time to talk. Only three things seemed to give me real peace in the middle of the night - listening to worship music on my iPod, prayer and reading my Bible.

Even though I hated the nights it was there in its quietness that I heard the voice of the Lord speak to me the most. During one of those moments I heard the words, "I will be faithful to do My part but you need to be faithful to do your part."

Then the story in Ezekiel 37 flashed into my thoughts. In his vision, Ezekiel was standing in the middle of a valley filled with dry human bones that were scattered as far as the eye could see. The bones represented Israel and all of the calamities and oppression that they had faced throughout their history.

The Lord asked Ezekiel, "Can theses bones live."

I love his response, "O Lord God, only you know."

In other words he was saying that he had no idea but he knew that God did.

Then the Lord told Ezekiel to prophesy over the bones and as he did the bones began to rattle and come together. Bones were flying through the air, colliding with each other and forming skeletons. Then ligaments, tendons, muscle and flesh formed on the skeletons. Right in front of Ezekiel's eyes the bones became bodies.

But one thing was lacking - life. The Lord then told Ezekiel to prophesy that breath would enter the bodies and when he did, the bodies came to life. The word here for breath, is pneuma, which is the same word used in the book of Genesis when God breathed life into Adam. In both cases we see bodies that were lifeless being brought to life.

The Lord then impressed on my heart to begin speaking this prophetic scripture over my body. Every night from then on when the hopelessness of my situation would begin to creep in, I would open my Bible and begin to read Ezekiel 37.

The doctors and the physical therapists were not giving me much hope, but the Creator of the human body gave me the only hope and assurance for healing that I needed, "Prophesy over these bones."

As I began to focus on the Word and on prayer, I didn't struggle nearly as much after everyone had gone home. After allowing God to become the center of my attention during the long nights of sleeplessness, I went from hating the night to excited anticipation of wondering what God would reveal to me this time.

Maybe you are going through a time in your life where the nights are filled with sleeplessness, anxiety, fear and hopelessness. In times like this the last thing you really want to do is to be still and listen. But I encourage you to do just that, stop, be quiet and listen to what the Lord wants to unveil to you in the still of the night. Open your Bible and see what He reveals to you as He gives you encouragement through His Word. It will bring new life and healing into your situation no matter what it may be. Don't give up!

Chapter 9

Hospital Hopping

Yet the Lord is faithful, and He will strengthen [you] and set you on a firm foundation and guard you from the evil [one].

-2 Thessalonians 3:3 AMP

I was admitted and discharged four times from the University of Iowa Hospital in Iowa City, Iowa, three times from the Davis County Hospital in Bloomfield, Iowa and twice from the Ottumwa Regional Hospital Ottumwa, Iowa.

I had also logged a lot of hours in the back of numerous different ambulances. I was truly impressed with the Davis County Ambulance crew. Not just for their kindness and professionalism but because before returning from Iowa City on one occasion they asked if I would mind if they stopped at a McDonald's after a long drive and wait at the hospital. I told them that would be fine and they even bought me a meal. How could I say no to that after living on hospital food for several weeks? So there we were going through a drive through in an ambulance (Even now while I write this, I'm smiling at the memory as I relive the moment).

I spent the first nine days after the accident on the trauma ward of the University of Iowa Hospital. It was a horrific time as I struggled with severe pain and the uncertainty of life itself. My nights were filled with sleeplessness and when I did finally doze off, I had constant nightmares. I was on one of the upper floors of the building facing the helicopter pad which seemed to be busy twenty-four hours a day. I would constantly watch them land and take off and pray for whoever was on each flight.

When I was stable enough, it was time to be transferred to what I thought would be my hometown hospital. That didn't happen. The Acute Rehabilitation Unit of the Ottumwa hospital had decided that due to the limitations of my condition and the need for multiple future surgeries, they at that time would not be able to meet my needs. We now had to decide between Cedar Rapids, Iowa which was even farther from Ottumwa, Fairfield, Iowa or Bloomfield, Iowa. Due to the closest proximity, we chose Bloomfield.

The amount of care and attention in a small town hospital with only a few patients compared to a crowded university hospital was immediately noticed. I felt like an instant celebrity.

As the days and nights blurred together and with sleep being a rarity due to the pain and discomfort of limited movement, I began to notice a pattern emerging. The nursing staff didn't just come in when my vitals needed checked but began to open up and share their personal lives and struggles with me. They were not only taking care of me but God was using me to minister to them.

During this whole ordeal I had determined that I was going to allow God to shine through my life and in my attitude no matter how much pain I was in or what the circumstances looked like. There were times that I had my meltdowns and moments of anger. I couldn't even go to the toilet without someone helping me sit on a bedpan and then wiping me after I had had a bowel movement. What a humbling and embarrassing experience.

As the days turned into weeks Jeff (not his real name) came into the room to check my vitals one night. He was very somber and hardhearted and the only nurse that I had not been able to connect with. All of a sudden as he was changing my IV he began to tell me that he had been raised in an abusive home by very religious parents. Because of this he was very angry and hostile towards Christians and all that they stood for.

I told him that I was very sorry for the abuse that he had endured as a child all in the name of "biblical discipline." I then began to share with him the true love of Jesus and to my surprise he listened intently. Before he left the room he turned to me and said, "You're different than any Christian I've ever met." I don't know what ever happened to Jeff after that, as not long after my discharge he moved to another town.

The next morning at 4 o'clock I was loaded back into an ambulance and transferred to the University of Iowa Hospital for another surgery. It was just a few days before

Christmas and my concerns weren't about the surgery but about where would we spend Christmas as a family.

Miriam had gotten a ride once again with Pastor Bill and they met my parents at the hospital. The plan was to operate on both legs but due to the severe swelling still in my foot only the left knee was ready for the long arduous procedure. My left tibia plateau had been shattered in what was estimated to be forty pieces. The smaller splinter sized pieces were removed and the larger bone fragments were set in place and screwed into the tibia with titanium screws. Then a six inch titanium plate was set against the bone fragments and my tibia and screwed into place for added support for my knee. The external fixator was then placed back on my leg from hip to ankle so that there would be no movement while my knee was healing.

I had lost a lot of blood during the procedure and once again my heart went into tachycardia as I lay in the recovery room. As I faded in-and-out of consciousness I wondered if I would ever see my family again.

We all waited in Dan's room this time to get an update on how the surgery went. Again, we waited for close to 6 hours and were getting anxious, worried and restless. Finally the nurse wheeled him into the room and apologized for the delay and informed us that they couldn't release him from the recovery room until his heart rate became normal. I always look back at that day as a day of another close encounter with death. My mum told me she had been praying for him at the time of the surgery, and felt deeply anxious, so she prayed until the anxiety lifted but it took awhile before it did. She called me right away to tell me what had happened to her and asked how Dan was. My mum was extremely worried and she didn't even know what had happened. I believe the Holy Spirit prompts his children to stand on behalf of those fighting a spiritual battle. On that day Dan was fighting once again for his life and Jesus pulled him through. Thank you Jesus!

I stayed all night, in the chair beside him. I didn't sleep at all - who can in those chairs? Dan was up most of the night too, in severe pain. I felt so bad for him; I wished I could have taken it all away.

After several hours I was finally stable enough to be transferred to a room. Suddenly in the middle of the night out of a sound, drug induced sleep; I was awakened by severe pain in my left leg. As I screamed out in agony every medical person who heard me came running in to see what had happened. Fearing that another blood clot had formed I was immediately tested. The results came back negative.

After two days I was loaded up once again in an ambulance and transported back to the Davis County Hospital where they had saved the exact room that I had been in for the previous three weeks. It was the longest and most painful, rough two hour drive I had ever experienced. The ride through the Rockies five years earlier was a leisurely ride compared to this. When we finally arrived back in Bloomfield I was actually excited as I was rolled back into my nice quiet room that had become my home-away-from-home.

Something was different though and the medical staff noticed it right away. I had normally been very upbeat and talkative and eager for whatever physical therapy was thrown at me. But now I was visibly weak and exhausted and could hardly lift my head off my pillow. As I drifted off to sleep I had a sense of excitement because tomorrow my family would be driving from as far as eight hours away to be with me at Christmas.

It was Saturday December 23rd. My family had always gotten together on the closest weekend to Christmas day to celebrate the birth of Christ. My parents, my brother Steve and his wife Carol, my nephew Mike and his wife Christy, my niece Bridget, my sister Vicki and her husband Rob, my brother-in-law William and of course Miriam, Caelan and Rian all were there. The hospital was very accommodating providing a large conference room for us to have our lunch and open gifts since there were too many of us to fit in the small room that I was in.

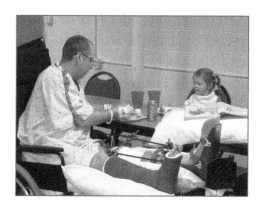

Christmas dinner with Caelan in the Davis County Hospital

It was a very tiring and emotional day. I was still feeling very weak and so after a few hours I excused myself and was wheeled back into my room. Once there, I wept.

After each family member said their goodbyes and Miriam and the kids drove the twenty miles back to Ottumwa, I felt more alone than ever. At that very moment a nurse came into the room and informed me that as they were going over my charts from Iowa City they noticed that an order had been given by the surgeon for me to have a blood transfusion before being transferred back to Bloomfield. For reasons that I will never know that transfusion never happened. No wonder I was so weak and tired. The Bible tells us that life is in the blood and after my transfusion I felt just that, alive.

The next day was Christmas Eve and I was disappointed that I hadn't been at home helping set up and decorate the tree, especially since this was Rian's first Christmas. I know he doesn't remember, but I sure do. I wasn't there to wrap the presents or stuff the stockings. I hadn't bought anything for Miriam before the accident happened so I told William to go buy her something and put my name on the box.

That night when a nurse came in to take my vitals I mentioned that it was probably going to be a long quiet night for the nursing staff. To my surprise the nurse went on to tell me that usually they were busy on that night because many elderly people who don't have any family would call 911 due to a mysterious illness and be admitted to the hospital just so that they didn't have to spend Christmas alone.

The thought of that broke my heart and spurred us to start a ministry where our church fills Christmas stockings and distributes them to hospitals and convalescent homes every year. My kids love to hand out the stockings because they know that no one should have to spend Christmas alone.

It was Christmas morning; never in our wildest dreams had we ever thought we would be having Christmas in a hospital. We were so thankful that we had Dan to celebrate Christmas with us. William, Caelan, Rian and I all jumped into the present laded car with our pajamas on and drove to the hospital. When we arrived we piled all the presents onto a wheel chair and wheeled them into Dan's room. He was very happy to see us and we spent all morning being buried under wrapping paper as the kids tore open their presents. We also had a family from the church deliver Christmas dinner to the hospital which made our day. They took time out of their Christmas to bring us food, what an amazing demonstration of the true meaning of the day.

When Miriam, William and the kids arrived they had so many presents that there almost wasn't enough room to put them all. A lot of people from our church had supported us financially, emotionally, prayerfully and, as I found out, with Christmas gifts for the kids. It was quite a scene watching them open their gifts. It wasn't the Christmas I envisioned having with my family, but I was so thankful that I was alive to see the joy in Caelan and Rian's faces as they opened each gift.

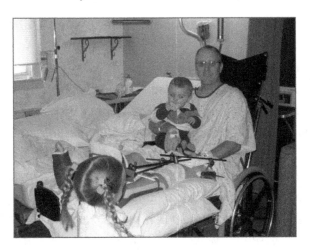

Two days later I left once again for Iowa City to have surgery on my right foot, only this time I would not be returning to Bloomfield. I had spent over a month there and the staff and I had become friends. I was sad that I wouldn't be back for the remainder of my recovery. I said my goodbyes and thanked each one of them as I was loaded in the Davis County ambulance one last time.

The surgery on my heel was by far more time consuming and detailed than my knee. On one occasion during the first few days after the accident, Doctor McKinley had told me that due to the complete shattering of my heal, he at that point had no idea what he was going to do to repair it. A typical shattered heel had large enough pieces to screw back together but mine was totally crushed.

Piece by piece the smaller bones were discarded and the larger ones put back into place with plates and screws. A cast was then placed on my leg and I was given a warning that if things didn't heal properly there would be a chance of amputation.

After two days in Iowa City I was transferred to the Acute Rehabilitation Unit of the Ottumwa Regional Hospital in Ottumwa, Iowa under the amazing care of Doctor Zahnle. She was one of the only physiatrists (doctor of rehabilitation) in the mid-west and of all the places for her to be employed; it was in our small town hospital!

I was once again extremely weak and exhausted upon arrival and this time I knew what those symptoms meant and asked if my records had indicated that I had suffered significant blood loss during my surgery. Once again in the post operative notes there was an order for a blood transfusion before I was discharged from the University of Iowa Hospital. I actually laughed this time at the fact that on two occasions this had gone unnoticed.

My first stay in Ottumwa Regional lasted two weeks. Since I was not able to put any weight on either leg for three more months my therapy only involved learning how to transfer from my bed to a wheelchair and back again. It was not as easy as I expected as it involved a lot of work to accomplish the transfer without bumping my legs.

It was during that week, while I was having one of my late night moments with the Lord, when all of a sudden the tormented screams of a young woman's voice pierced the quietness of the night. Suddenly I saw the person the voice belonged to run past my room with a number of nurses in hot pursuit. Once they captured her she was taken back to her room where a nurse was placed as a guard at her door so that she wouldn't be able to leave her room again. They may have stopped her from leaving her room but the tormented screams continued night after night.

On one night when the nurse came in to take my vitals I asked what this girl's story was. She told me that she had been in a car accident in which she was not wearing a seat belt and she had sustained severe brain damage. As the screams continued the Holy Spirit began to reveal to me that just as I had been tormented with nightmares and demonic visions during the first few nights after my accident that this girl too was suffering the same. At that moment I prayed that deliverance and peace would fill her mind and body and instantly there was quiet. For the rest of my stay she was a model patient - the nurses told me that they had no idea what had happened to cause such a drastic change!

At the end of my first week on the Acute Rehabilitation Unit Doctor Zahnle informed me that as soon as our house was made ready for my arrival, which included a wheelchair ramp, I would be released to go home. We had no idea who to contact about building the ramp but as the word was extended to our church about the need, a group of men came over on a cold January morning and in one day completed not only a functional wheelchair ramp but one that was also beautifully constructed.

Two days before Rian's first birthday I was discharged and for the first time in nearly two months I was about to return to the scene of the accident. I was both excited and apprehensive. I was excited that I would be in my own home with my family and apprehensive that I would no longer have a trained medical professional at my side day or night if I had a concern.

No matter how anxious I felt, I was finally going to be home with my wife and my children.

I have always celebrated birthdays with a bang! The day is all about you and I want to make sure to you feel special on that day. Caelan's first birthday was BIG! We were all huddle like sardines in a can for her birthday party but she loved it- I loved it! For Rian's birthday, he got a dairy – free, soy- free chocolate muffin with a candle in it - that was like eating a rock! He sat with a party hat on, munching this terrible cake opposite Dan who was confined to a hospital bed. Even though it was hard for me that we never threw a big party for his 1st, little did he know that he had the best birthday gift anyone could ever have - to have his Daddy home, alive!

Chapter 10

Rise Up and Walk

In the name of Jesus Christ of Nazareth, rise up and walk.
-Acts 3:6 NKJV

It was great to have Dan home! William and I had transformed our dining room into a bedroom since our bedroom was in the basement, making it inaccessible for Dan. A hospital bed was set up where the dining room table had once been and since every other room in the house could only be accessed through the dining room, we strung a curtain from one side of the room to the other so that Dan could have some privacy.

Our house was not handicapped accessible at all. It was a 900 square foot two bedroom house with very narrow doorways, old heavy storm doors and stairs. I have never really got into D.I.Y but I had to make some changes before Dan was able to come home. I called a few of his friends and asked for some help. The church was fantastic at helping me out with anything I needed. We needed a ramp built for the front steps due to Dan being in a wheelchair, so the church men got together and built the most awesome ramp. The Doctor was pretty amazed at it too. She drove by it once, and she was shocked that they built it for free! You can do more witnessing by your actions than your words! Pushing Dan up and down the ramp was very difficult and picking up the wheelchair to put in the van was not fun either; I am 5 feet tall and weigh 112 pounds but I did it!

Now that Dan was home, life was a bit more hectic than it had been since the accident. He needed help with a lot of daily things that he used to do for himself. I had a lot on my plate so thank the Lord we had my brother, William, living with us at that time.

The transition from hospital to home was much more difficult than I had imagined. The dining room had a large picture window facing the back yard and the spot where I had landed when I fell off of the roof. I found myself continually staring at that spot. As the tears streamed down my face, I wished that I had December 3 2006 to do all over again.

I would also look out and watch Miriam and William pull Caelan and Rian around on the sled and build snowmen in the fresh winter snow. One worry that haunted me was that I might never again be able to enjoy moments like that with my children. I kept reminding myself of the words that I had heard the Holy Spirit speak to me - God had promised that He would do His part and I was also determined that I would do mine so that one day I would get to play with my children once again.

It had been six weeks since my final surgery and the time had come to return to Iowa City, this time to the orthopedic clinic instead of the hospital. The paramedics arrived at the house early in the morning and lifted me onto the gurney and loaded me once again into the back of an ambulance. This was my seventh trip over the previous three months so I had gotten used to the ride.

Being pleased with the healing of my left knee Doctor McKinley decided that it was time to remove the external fixator. One of the medical students was doing his rotation in the orthopedics department got the order to remove the brace after Doctor McKinley gave him a quick lesson on how it was to be done. I don't know who was more nervous, me or him!

The six inch titanium screws were then removed from my hip and lower leg without any numbing agent and by using a manual ratchet to back them out of the bone and muscle. I can't say that it was a painful procedure but I definitely would not want to ever go through it again. Since my knee had been immobilized for so long, I was not able to bend it at all when the fixator was removed. It was now time for the physical therapy to begin.

Since I was still unable to put any weight on either leg until the shattered bones had completely healed my therapy consisted of trying to regain mobility and strength in my left knee. A physical therapist came over to the house three times a week to guide me through the exercises. I was not prepared for the amount of pain and hard work that I was about to endure.

My knee was locked in place and no matter how hard I tried I could not move it even one inch. The therapist's solution was to force it to move. She would grab my ankle and gently but firmly push down stretching the ligaments and tendons. The first few sessions I screamed like a little girl. In fact, three year old Caelan would become so upset at this stranger hurting her daddy that she would always cry so Miriam had to take her elsewhere for every therapy session.

After several weeks of constant work and pain I could only move my knee ten degrees. It was hardly noticeable. How frustrating! Over the next two weeks as the therapist measured the bend in my knee it increased to twenty degrees, then thirty. It seemed that I was finally making progress.

One day Miriam had a lady from our church approach her and tell her that her husband, Josh, was the head trainer for the William Penn University athletics department and he wanted to know if he could help me with my physical therapy. Josh and I hit it off right from the start but his approach to therapy was geared towards college athletes and was much more intense than what I had been used to. However, I was determined to do whatever it took to walk again.

On the very first night that Josh came over he asked me if I was tired of being confined to a bed and a wheelchair. I didn't even have to think about my answer because after three months without the use of my legs and only being able to fit my wheelchair through two of the doorways in the house I was more than tired of being confined. I gained such a respect for those who are bound to beds and wheelchairs. They are truly heroic people in my eyes.

What I didn't realize when Josh had asked me that question was that he had a plan. He looked at me with a smile and asked if I would like to learn how to lower and raise myself in and out of the wheelchair. He then added that if I did I would be able to scoot along the floor into the other rooms and then lift myself into a chair or onto another bed. I was very nervous but I practiced raising and lowering myself from the wheelchair to the floor and then back into the wheelchair until my arms were too tired to continue. The first place I scooted to was the bathroom where I raised myself onto the toilet. After using a bedpan for the previous three months I truly did feel like I was sitting on a throne.

Since the accident the only way I was able to wash was a sponge bath, so the second thing I wanted to do was to sit in the bathtub. I would lift myself into the empty tub to make sure that the cast on my right leg wouldn't get wet, hang the leg over the edge of the tub and then fill it up with water. These two things that most of us take for granted had now become a great accomplishment in my effort to regain any sense of normality that I could.

But the best thing about being able to lower myself onto the floor was that for the first time in three months, I was able to play with my children. If God had not placed Josh into my life I know that my recovery would have lasted much longer.

Four months after my accident, the time came to have my cast removed from my right leg. After the x-rays revealed complete healing of the bones, I was now ready to begin the most difficult part of my physical therapy - learning to walk again.

I was admitted back into the Acute Rehabilitation Unit in Ottumwa for ten days. I once again would develop a bond with a whole new group of medical professionals that has lasted to this very day.

To the vast majority of us walking comes easily. Face it; we really don't think about how we walk - we just walk. For my job as a meter reader I walked between six and ten miles a day but it had not only been over four months since I took my last step, it had been that long since I had even stood on my feet. My first exercise was learning how to stand all over again. It had only been a few months earlier that, Rian had taken his first steps so I envisioned myself as a forty-two year old toddler learning to walk.

When I played high school football practice prior to the start of school included two-a-day sessions, two hours in the morning and two hours in the afternoon. My hospital physical therapy treatment would also include a morning and afternoon session which would make football practice seem like a leisurely stroll.

When the therapist came in for my first session she attached a gait belt around my waist which was there in case I stumbled as it would give her something to grab hold of to keep me from falling. A walker was placed next to the bed and for the first time since the accident I put my feet on the floor, grabbed hold of the walker and stood up.

I have always had pencil thin legs but after four months of inactivity my legs had atrophied and they looked more like pencil leads, skin on bone. I couldn't believe how difficult it was as I stood there with most of my body weight being held up with my arms on the walker. After a few minutes of standing I lay back in bed and we worked on the flexibility of my knee. Just those few minutes on my feet were exhausting.

In the afternoon session I pulled myself up on the walker once again. This time the therapist told me that I would be walking as far down the hall as I could and then return back to my room. I couldn't believe that I had to tell myself mentally to put one leg in front of the other heel-to-toe. I took forty steps down the hall and then turned around and went back to my bed.

On the third day I began learning how to walk with crutches which gave even more mobility. In the afternoon session I was taken to a flight of stairs and told that the time had come to learn how to go up and down stairs using my crutches. I was terrified! What if I fell? The thought of getting injured again had always been in the back of my mind. With a lot of persuasion and encouragement I ascended and then descended six steps. I did it! I actually could move around without a wheelchair but I was far from being able to walk without support.

After ten days on the Acute Rehabilitation Unit I was released to go home. I would continue to take outpatient physical therapy for the next five months before I would finally be able to walk without the assistance of crutches or a cane.

We lived right next door to the high school football field and as a part of my therapy I would walk around the track with the aid of a cane. When I first started this routine, the tears would stream down my face due to the pain and frustration as I made my laps around the track. As the days turned into weeks the pain and frustration slowly began to fade. I would walk a mile each day which was tiring and difficult so I had no idea if I would be able to walk the six to ten miles a day that my job required and in all types of terrains and weather conditions.

It had been nearly ten months since the accident had happened and with my scheduled monthly examination a few days away, I would find out when and if I would return to work. Doctor McKinley decided that I was ready to attempt half days and then went on to say that if I felt I was unable to do the job, he would sign the paperwork so that I could collect disability.

I would like to say that my return to work was easy, but it wasn't. Every few blocks I would stop and sit on the steps of someone's house. There were times I wept because the pain, exhaustion and frustration where overwhelming. But I also knew that the promise I received on that quiet and lonely night in a hospital bed had now been fulfilled. God had done His part and I was trying my hardest to do mine.

Chapter 11

Walking in a Cave Without a Light

Then I said to myself, "Oh, he even sees me in the dark!
At night I'm immersed in the light!" It's a fact: darkness isn't
dark to you; night and day, darkness and light,
they're all the same to you.
-Psalms 139:11-12 The Message

Have you ever been in a cave? One of my fondest memories as a child was when my parents loaded us in the car every summer and off we went on our family vacation which spanned at least thirty states by the time I was eighteen. On several of those trips we toured massive caves in Colorado and in Tennessee.

It was on one of those adventures that the guide pointed out the signs that told all who entered to stay on the marked paths for our safety. Caves, even ones that are on display for tourists, are dangerous.

As we descended deep into the cave the tour guide asked us all to stand completely still as the lights in the cave were turned off for maybe thirty seconds. A collective gasp filled the air and I felt my body begin to sway from the sudden equilibrium shift caused by the complete darkness. As a ten year old I instantly felt fear as my mind began to fantasize about what creatures might be lurking in the dark.

The reason the tour guide had told us to stand completely still was because she knew that in the complete darkness of the cave, a person could easily become disoriented, lose their balance and fall. Caves are full of rubble, small and large rocks and holes. Without a light to illuminate your path, one wrong step could mean injury and even death.

When we are surrounded by total darkness even in the most familiar place our minds can play tricks on us and all of our irrational fears can paralyze us.

It was at this point in my recovery that I began to experience the effects of walking in a cave without a light due to my chronic pain and lack of mobility. The darkness of severe depression and anxiety began to envelop me. It did not happen quickly like the tour guide shutting off the light. It was more as if I had walked into the mouth of the cave and began the slow decent into the darkness. It started out as frustration at being confined to a bed and then a wheelchair. My entire life I have been very active. Sports, recreation and my job, reading waters meters were the norm. I had gone from being self sufficient to having someone help me roll onto a bedpan so that I could defecate then wipe me and help me roll off it.

Even though God had miraculously met every one of our needs up to this point, instead of turning around and heading back toward the light of the cave's entrance, something about the dark drew me into its grasp. I quickly spiraled into depression and hopelessness and even thoughts of suicide. It was as if a sudden cave-in had blocked my only way out and there I was trapped in total darkness and despair.

I would wake up in the middle of the night drenched in sweat and gasping for air as nightmares and panic consumed my mind once again. Fears of never walking again, death and the deaths of my parents, wife and children tormented me. I would cry out to God and my fears would slowly fade as I drifted off to sleep until the next nightmare and panic attack came. The process would start all over again, night after endless night, leading to days of deeper depression and hopelessness.

Two events happened that caused me to seek help. The first happened while our kids were playing on the floor of our living room. One year old Rian walloped Caelan (who was three) on the side of the head with one of his toys. She screamed and cried and I reacted in an irrational fit of rage. I hobbled over to Rian yelling as I went, grabbed his toy and broke it! Did the punishment fit the crime? Not even close. Being naturally laid back in my personality, I was shocked at my response.

In the darkness of the cave even the smallest pebble can cause you to trip and fall. I wish I could say that after that episode I did not react irrationally again but in reality it was the first of many reactions to trivial irritants.

The second episode that caused me to seek help involved my three year old daughter Caelan. It was seven months after the accident and I was able to drive once again. I took Caelan out to run an errand with me and at one point, for reasons I can't remember, she started crying at the top of her lungs. After about a minute of trying to calm her as we drove down the road, I completely lost it. I began shouting, "Shut up! Shut up! Shut up!" so loudly my voice went hoarse.

Right then I knew that I needed help. I called my pastor and he gave me the name of a Christian counselor in Des Moines, Iowa who worked for Kavalier and Associates. It was decided that the best course of action to help me through this cave experience was to begin taking medication. In America, you may have seen the commercials whose catch phase is, "When depression hurts." Mine definitely hurt and typically I would have fought the idea of taking an anti-depressant due to my pride, thinking I could handle this myself. But I knew that this time, I was outmatched and agreed to try it.

There seems to be a stigma for people on antidepressants and even more so for those who are Christians. Somehow we feel that if we need medical attention or the help of medicine for our lives to be healed, our faith is weak and we have failed as a follower of Christ. This is farthest from the truth. If you were swept away by flood waters would refuse the help of a rescuer? I really don't think any one of us would say, "Sorry, but I'm waiting for God to pull me out of the raging waters and if I allow you to save me that would be a lack of faith on my part."

Who are we to tell God what method He can use to bring us healing? He may use a miracle or medicine and in many cases including my own, he used both.

After two weeks on the medication there was a dramatic reduction in pain and my mental outlook vastly improved.

If you are struggling with the fact that you need to take medication to bring physical or mental healing into your life, please allow God to use whatever method He chooses. No matter what method is used to restore your life, the One who is in control and will always be in control of your situation is God.

I am no longer on antidepressants as the healing process in that area of my life has reached full circle. I still get down at times like we all do, but now I am able to cope with the help of the Holy Spirit.

I went on and came off of the medications under the watchful eye of the physicians and counselors and I advise all who feel God has healed them and who want to come off of any mediation, to make sure you do so with the consent of your physician. There is nothing more powerful than a physician's confirmation of the healing power of Jesus.

Chapter 12

More than Enough

O Lᴏʀᴅ my God, you have performed many wonders for us.
Your plans for us are too numerous to list.
You have no equal.
If I tried to recite all your wonderful deeds,
I would never come to the end of them.
-Psalms 40:5 NLT

The Bible tells us that God is able to supply all of our needs according to His riches. We were about to live out that scripture.

During the first three months of the accident, I never had to cook for the family because our church provided every meal. At Christmas Caelan and Rian received 2 huge bags of presents. If we had a need, it was met. We were truly blown away by the support and help we received from First Church of the Open Bible, Ottumwa, from friends and family. You have shown the very essence of Jesus' ministry, to love and care for those in need. You will always have a special place in our hearts. Thank you for your love.

What a great example of how the church should function. In fact one of my favorite passages of scripture is Acts 2:42-47 where the early church was not just content sitting in a church service but they sought out those who had a need so that they could offer help and boy did we have a lot of needs!

I had only been home a few weeks when I got a letter in the mail from our insurance company informing me the Water Works policy was that once an employee was off work for six consecutive weeks their insurance would automatically be terminated. The letter went on to say that if I wanted to continue my coverage I would have to pay $1,500 a month. There was no possible way we could afford to do that.

I immediately called the Water Works office manager to plead my case. Once I explained the details of the letter she admitted that she didn't realize that the policy existed. After confirming it to be factual she met with Richard Wilcox who was the general manager at that time.

A special session of the board was convened and a vote was taken to amend the policy so that my premiums would continue to be paid. The vote was unanimous. Not only was my insurance continued but out of the over $250,000 of medical bills that we had accrued over my recovery; we had to pay only $4,000 of it. We had seen Jesus perform the physically miraculous in my life and now we were experiencing the financial.

As the weeks turned into months and my vacation and sick leave began to dwindle down to just a few days we had no idea how we would be able to pay our bills and buy food once my pay ceased. I kept getting these flashes in my head of the AFLAC duck and wishing that I had been covered by them too. But Jesus was about to prove faithful once again because He has promised in His Word that if He takes care of the flowers of the field and the birds of the air how much more will He take care of us, His children.

We had received money from numerous people in our church and from our church organization (Open Bible Churches) and the Northgate Alliance Church in town had somehow heard of our situation and sent us a check for two hundred and fifty dollars. What a model of a church hearing of a need and then doing what they can to help.

As much as every penny helped, without a weekly income we had no idea how we would pay our mortgage, let alone other bills. Gary, one of my coworkers, knowing that our situation was about to become financially drastic, asked if he could donate some of his vacation time to me so that we would have some income. Not only was he allowed to donate time but all the employees were given the opportunity to donate sick leave or vacation time so that we would not be without an income. This was yet another first in the over one hundred years existence of the Ottumwa Water Works.

In the ten months that I was off work, not only did I not miss a single pay check but I had five weeks of sick time remaining when I was released to go back to work. With all of my continued appointments with the orthopedic surgeon in Iowa City and the days that I needed to take off to rest my legs, I needed every one of them.

Most of us are very familiar with the story in Matthew 14 where a boy gave his lunch of five loaves of bread and two small fish to Jesus so that five thousand hungry men plus women and children could be fed. Can you imagine not only the disciples' reaction but that of the boy when his little lunch became twelve baskets of leftovers?

The Bible doesn't tell us what became of the leftovers, but I imagine that the boy took home more than he came with. Many of the people had walked long distances to hear Jesus and perhaps they were given food to take with them on the journey home. Perhaps the disciples took the leftovers to the poor. I am sure that the food wasn't wasted and it served a purpose. My leftover time off also served a purpose.

Now that our finances were taken care of my future employment was still in question. The doctors and the physical therapists were telling me that there was a very good chance that my legs would not be able to endure the punishment of walking six to ten miles a day over various terrains and in the ice and snow of winter.

With this a possibility I was asked to meet with the Water Works board to discuss my future. I was still on crutches which was an improvement from the wheelchair that I was confined to on the previous meeting with them. Miriam and I were both very nervous as we sat there not knowing what to expect. I don't know why we were because Jesus had provided one miracle after another and He wasn't about to let us down now.

As we sat there, every board member encouraged and affirmed us and once again agreed unanimously that no matter how long my recovery took, my job would be there waiting for me when I was able to return. Three months later I walked through the doors, clocked in and began my work day for the first time in nine months.

I would like to say that the first few weeks were easy but it was far from that. With every step that I took on the uneven ground (I had only walked on paved surfaces and floors up to this point) the pain was almost unbearable. About every block I would stop and sit on the steps of the house of the meter I had just read and rest and pray that the Lord would help me. I was beginning to wonder if the doctor was right and I would no longer be able to do my job.

As the days turned into weeks, then months and now five years later as we right this book, through the heat of summer and the cold and snow of winter the pain and limitations began to decrease. I still struggle with pain and some limitations but I have never missed a day of work due to my injuries. God has truly been my strength when I felt so weak.

Perhaps you have had people say to you as some still do to me, "If you had more faith you wouldn't have any limitations and pain." At first those words would anger or hurt me. But as I prayed about "complete healing" the Holy Spirit reminded me of what the Apostle Paul said in 2 Corinthians 12:8-10 (The Message),

"Three times I did that (prayed) and then he told me, My grace is enough; it's all you need. My strength comes into its own in your weakness. Once I heard that, I was glad to let it happen. I quit focusing on the handicap and began appreciating the gift. It was a case of Christ's strength moving in on my weakness. Now I take limitations in stride, and with good cheer, these limitations that cut me down to size—abuse, accidents, opposition, bad breaks. I just let Christ take over! And so the weaker I get, the stronger I become."

It is frustrating at times as I face my new normal, but it serves as a reminder of what could have been and of the miracle that God did perform. Be encouraged that God is still at work in your life as He is in mine. I am not one who believes that I can tell God what He should and should not do and since I still have this "thorn in my flesh" I know that God will use it to bring glory to Himself if I allow it through my attitude and actions.

As for those who make statements like that-typically they have not faced the reality of what you and I are going through or they are bitter and disappointed because God didn't come through in a way that they expected so they are unable to grasp the magnitude of what God has done and is doing in our lives and how we can rejoice in the midst of it.

I don't know why our story has turned out the way that it did or why so many others have ended in disappointment and even tragedy. Sometimes life doesn't make sense and I am not even going to begin to try and explain why God does what He does, because I can't. Sin brought pain and death into the world and until death is thrown in the lake of fire at the final judgment it will rule this world. When that day happens, death, pain and sorrow will no longer exist. Until then we must always remember that God knows what pain, loss and death are all about as He exchanged His Son's life for your life and mine.

One day I know that we will all know the answers to every question and on that day we will all receive our complete healing; that day will be when we live with Jesus in Heaven in our heavenly, perfect bodies and be reunited with the loved ones who have gone on before us...never to be separated again – what a beautiful day that's going to be!

Chapter 13

Hidden Brokenness

If your heart is broken, you'll find God right there;
if you're kicked in the gut, he'll help you catch your breath.
-Psalm 34:18 The Message

I know Dan and I have talked a lot about our own events and situations which have challenged and formed us. We had a choice: to add to our brokenness or to allow God to restore us.

Dan was forced to deal with his condition; he had nowhere to hide (physically and emotionally) like a lot of us who experience things that happen unexpectedly. He experienced events that caused his brokenness to be exposed, he had to face it, deal with it and move on. Don't get me wrong, he still struggles and tries to work through emotional and especially physical issues. He lives with chronic pain and has scars that remind him daily of what he went through. One of the worst reactions to brokenness is ignoring it. Dan's outcome would have been completely different if he would have ignored the reality of his injuries. We have all heard the expression, "Time is a good healer "which is true, but it is how you use that time which determines the outcome of your healing. You can't physically see it but it leaves footprints where it has been.

For years I battled emotional and mental torment from past issues, and those, I later found out were connected to my family and my birth. Problems that may be very simple but if you leave them long enough to fester, they can cause a lot of damage! Through most of my childhood and teenage life, I struggled with academics, confidence and self-esteem like so many do. I felt like I was a BIG cut below normal! I remember getting to a point saying, "I can't be normal! There something wrong with me!" It became so bad, I decided at the age of 21, to get tested for hearing and learning difficulties after struggling to earn my degree. When they tested me they found out I had a serious hearing impairment.

Since I was born in the Jungle, there were no doctors to immediately test me for all sorts of things like they do in the western world. The doctors simply assumed that I have had it from birth.

Everyone has been amazed at what I have accomplished with so little hearing! I did a good job of pretending in life because of the embarrassment of it but I felt like I had accomplished very little. I continually felt dumb, stupid and that I wouldn't mount to much! Ironically, my negative self-talk and insults from others, which I carried around for years, somehow gave me comfort even though I hurt emotionally and physically because I suppressed them.

I had formed so many lies in my head about myself that I believed them all to be true! I longed to be healed but wanted to be left alone. I didn't know what to do! My reaction to it was to turn my head away from it all because it just hurt too much, so

I simply "swallowed it back down." When the problems surfaced I would abruptly cut off the conversation or prayer that caused it to arise.

I was so hurt and angry at God for years about our honeymoon, about my separation from my family and other issues. Ever since the day I left my family to come to the States (which is where I call home now), I felt my family where all dead to me. A terrible thought I know! But that's how I felt. I started progressively having panic attacks and abandonment issues at the thought of them. It got to the point where I didn't even want to talk to them on the phone because it hurt so badly; I just wanted to be with them.

Now you are probably thinking right now, well, if you feel that bad just move back and get over it, right? The fact is I truly love the Unites States and the people here! I know this is where I am meant to be. I have always felt like an American trapped in a Northern Irish body! So when I'm in the States, I miss Northern Ireland and when I am in Ireland, I miss the States. I can never win! But I knew it wasn't normal for a person to react this strongly about leaving their family. I continually ignored it all until it got to the point when it started to over flow and I couldn't control it any longer.

I felt God was very silent in those years but I now realize that I was the one who was silent. Truthfully, I look back now and realize all of the emotions that I felt were connected to ones that already were rooted so deeply within me and the situation I was now in just revealed them. Yet I continued to dismiss the turmoil I was living inside.

I love watching the National Geographic channel about nature and I have seen episodes about animals that get inside of other animal (or human) bodies and eat them alive! I know it sounds seriously gross but in a way that's what I felt happened to me, slowly, being eaten alive by the hurt, loneliness, insecurity and abandonment issues. I couldn't do anything about it and I felt controlled by it. They had all made themselves a nice comfortable home in my life. All the "stuff and pieces" I carried distorted my view of myself, my relationships and God!

It took me ten years, 10 YEARS of praying and asking the Lord for forgiveness for holding on to all this sin because truthfully that's what it was! I asked continually for Him to bring about my healing in some way because I couldn't give it to Him, it was just too painful. I would sit; just sit in His Presence asking Him to heal me inside. In many ways, I would have saved myself a lot of years if I had just given it to Him but the hurt was too real and I didn't want to face it.

Slowly, year by year He would reveal things in my life which needed to be restored. I remember being prompted by the Holy Spirit to clean out what I had collected inside. I made a decision to go and talk to a Christian counselor, although I am not a great fan of talking to people about my private life in general but I felt that I needed extra help to understand the things that didn't add up.

I look back and see the footprints of the Holy Spirit over the last ten years of my life as He has revealed and restored all of my broken pieces. A new and more whole me! It took me to stop looking at what had happened and to start seeing His work in it! I still have a lot to clean up and I don't believe we should stop cleaning and searching ourselves until we are in Jesus' presence face to face. I think sometimes we give up too early or finish our ongoing search for inner wholeness because it isn't going according to our schedule.

We are all broken, with a need to embrace that brokenness, no matter how long it takes. God longs for us to be in union with Him, to have a daily involvement in our lives. He sees us as whole, perfected, restored and changed people and He wants us to see ourselves that way too. When we live with Him and walk with Him, it is impossible not to be changed, renewed and restored. The God that never changes, changes everything He touches.

Who do we think we are kidding when we try to hide our broken pieces and baggage? We definitely are not kidding God because He looks at the heart. It is just like going back to the Garden of Eden, when Adam and Eve sinned. They hid from God and were separated from Him, even though they hid themselves, God knew where they were and what they had done.

I think that the biggest lie is that we just want to be alone with all of our "stuff "and we don't want anyone to mess with it or get involved with it. We just want to hide! This is totally opposite to how we can receive true freedom. We need to hand it over to the Creator who can put us back together. He creates a new you! Only in Him we become a new creation, the old has gone, new has come (2 Corinthians 5:17).

The only way we can achieve that is by doing what we were made to do: walk with God! We are created to have an intimate relationship with Him and to be in continual communication with Him. Without Him we are nothing.

In those early days, when God created Adam, the human race walked with God. Can you imagine that? Can you hear the sound of God walking beside you? Adam walked with his Creator and had an intimate relationship, like no other relationship in the garden. God provided everything for him and then told him to dwell in and govern His beautiful creation. He had no qualifications for the job other than that was what God had created him to do. God simply made him and loved him and cared for him just as He does you and me. When Adam and Eve ate from the forbidden fruit, they became separated from God and from that day on we all became broken and the only answer to that brokenness is Jesus.

John 3:16 tells us that God sent his only Son, Jesus Christ to amend that distance between us, so that we may once again walk with Him, have fellowship with Him, be healed and live with Him for eternity. Can you imagine the sheer thought of how much God loves us for Him to do that for us? But what we tend to forget is that when we ask Jesus into our lives we think that's it….. Life is great….. God's got me…..but it's not supposed to end there. It seems like we treat God like another App to add to our other organized Apps on our phone or another insurance policy we pay into every month to make sure we are covered. No, He wants more than "I do"; He longs to be infused with every part of our lives. Then that causes us to affect others just by living life.

We were created to walk with Him and to hear His voice in a broken world. Whenever we choose not to walk in His presence, we feel the consequences of that lack of intimacy and will not only continue to be broken but we will add to that brokenness. Our condition will not be healed. Only the One who breathed life into our lungs and made us can put us back together, inside and outside. But we must be obedient and willing to give Him the first piece. That was a difficult choice for me to make and I am so thankful that with His strength working in me, I was able to hand Him the first piece.

Chapter 14

Not the End

No eye has seen, no ear has heard,
and no mind has imagined
what God has prepared
for those who love him.
                    -1 Corinthians 2:9 NLT

This may be the last chapter in this book but it's definitely not the end. It is not the end for us and it is not the end for you.

Many years have passed since that fateful day and I do still battle chronic pain, physical limitation and even emotional meltdowns once in awhile. But each one of those moments is a reminder that our story could have had a completely different ending.

One of my biggest concerns during the healing process was that I would never get to play with my children again. I rarely have missed a day of play with my children since I became mobile. We play tag, soccer, softball, go swimming and in the winter I pull them around on a sled and build snow forts and snowmen. I get on the floor and play dolls and Lego and I do a great Darth Vader imitation as we run around the house and battle for the galaxy playing Star Wars. I may not be able to run as fast or get up and down off of the floor like I did pre-accident but God gave me the desire of my heart to play with my children as they grow up.

I also get to hold my wife's hand as we stroll on the beaches and through the ancient castles of Northern Ireland and as we walk on the sidewalks of our neighborhood.

*Gerald (Miriam's dad) Miriam, Dan, Rian and Caelan at Carrickfergus
Castle in Northern Ireland*

I wondered if I would ever get to do these simple
things again in the early stages of my recovery...the
answer was yes I would.

God has also used this accident to reach people with
the love of Jesus whom I would have never gotten to meet.
It opened the door to serve on the Ottumwa Regional
Hospital's Acute Physical Rehabilitation board for two
years where I was able to recommend changes through
my experience.

When the doctors had patients who were on the verge
of giving up on their therapy, I was invited to come and
share my story and encourage them to continue. We have
shared our story in churches where we have gotten the
privilege to pray for people and rejoice over the testimonies
of God's healing power.

I have also gotten to pray with my doctor, who is of
the Muslim faith. As I prayed the tears streamed down
her cheeks as the Holy Spirit ministered to her. I would
have never met her if it weren't for my accident.

I served as the co-facilitator for a physical rehabilitation support group for one year, sharing how the healing power of Jesus played a huge role in my recovery.

We have found that through our brokenness God has used it and us to bring healing to other people. You too can use your experience to bring healing and hope to the lives of others by telling your story of the faithfulness of Jesus in your life.

When God had placed it on our hearts to write this book we knew that it was for the purpose of encouraging those of you who are facing a difficult time in your life. Life is difficult at times but we hope to remind you through our story that Jesus is right there with you just as He was and still is with us. We may never get the opportunity to talk to or pray for you face to face, but we would still love to hear your story and pray for you. You can reach us on Facebook at Broken Healer or on our website at www. danandmiriampope.com. We may not be able to contact every one of you, but know that everyone who needs prayer will receive it. You will also be able to watch videos and see pictures of our adventure.

We encourage you to sit at the Lord's feet and ask the Holy Spirit to show you any brokenness or hurt that is holding you back from living life to the fullness, the way God intends you to live. As you pray the prayer below watch as the Healer begins healing your life.

A Prayer for the Broken

Dear Jesus,

Thank You for being obedient to the point of allowing Yourself to be broken so that I would receive healing through the beating You endured and the blood that You shed. Thank You for Your unconditional love for me.

Today, I willingly give You the pieces of my brokenness and ask You to forgive me of my sin and selfishness. I can't put them back together myself and need Your help to become whole and healed once again. I give permission for You to search me as I hand You every piece; some will be very difficult for me to hand over to You so please help me to let them go. I understand it will take time and I commit my days of healing into Your hands, understanding that it will come in Your perfect time and way. I know that You have already done what You have promised and I promise to do my part too.

I ask this in Jesus name.
Amen

End Notes

Foreword

1. Rend Collective Experiment. "Faithful." Organic Family Hymnal. Survivor Records, 2010. www.rendcollectiveexperiment.com

Chapter 1

2. Stamphill, Ira. "*I* Know Who Holds Tomorrow." *(1950)*